YOUR WRITE TO HEAL

Transformation
Through Writing

Your Write to Heal

Transformation Through Writing

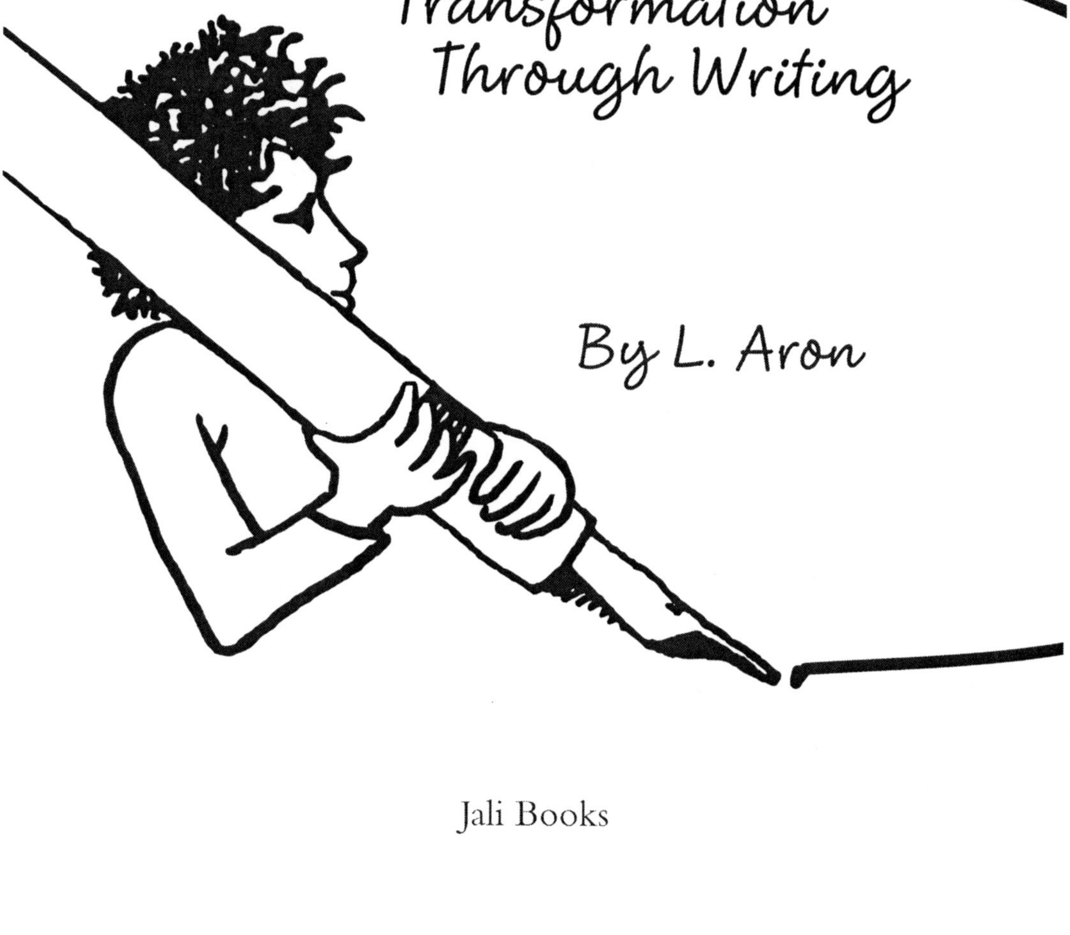

By L. Aron

Jali Books

Jali Books

Library of Congress Catalog Card Number: LCCN 2011901457

Aron, L.
Your Write to Heal: A Guide to Transformation Through Writing / L. Aron
ISBN 978-1-934639-07-8

Design and Typography by Marc Morrell
Cover Illustration by Ilene Frischer
Photograph of the author © 2010 Felicia Lebow, www.photographybyfelicia.com

Printed in the United States of America

Imprint: Jali Books

CONTENTS

ACKNOWLEDGEMENTS

I used to think that writing a book was a solitary experience. Now I know that the work is woven with the golden support of loved ones, the smiles of strangers and the crystalline tears of experience. I am very thankful and grateful for the love, patience and wisdom of those around me, especially when the words didn't flow and the spirit was weak.

The idea for this book originally came from my work at Gilda's Club in New York City where I have been teaching monthly writing workshops since the facility opened in 1995. The club was named for Gilda Radner, one of television's most beloved comediennes from the original days of **Saturday Night Live**.

She was fearless, comical and approachable. Ovarian cancer was unstoppable at that time, and many viewers felt as if they were losing a close friend when they heard the news that Gilda was battling the disease. As part of her treatment she had seen the gifted therapist Joanna Bull who demonstrated the impact that emotional and psychological support can have on patients, their friends and relatives. As Radner made peace with her situation she felt that her legacy should be the creation of places where people affected by the disease could be supported and nurtured.

In 1995, six years after Gilda's death, her beloved husband, the ever-fabulous actor Gene Wilder, and Ms. Bull announced the opening of the flagship Gilda's Club in New York City. "The Mission is to create welcoming communities of free support for everyone living with cancer-men, women, teens and children-along with their families and friends. Their innovative program is an essential complement to medical care, providing networking and support groups, workshops, education and social activities." (www.gildasclubnyc.org). There is no fee to belong and all the workshops are taught by volunteers. The guidance and inspiration offered has proven to be so crucial to healing that there are now clubs nationwide and abroad. Gilda's remarkable energy still infuses the clubhouses. I am awed by the strength and courage of the people who attend the workshops. Some of the writing in this book comes from members who have graciously shared their stories. I have witnessed miracles there and am pleased to be donating a portion of the proceeds from this book to the club.

I also have been encouraged, mentored, educated, loved and nudged by some blessed professionals along the way. Dr. Robert Goldblatt's practical and profound advice is generously shared throughout this text. Dr. Rick Munter's caring, generosity and willingness to keep a bargain allowed for ever-expanding consciousness. Barbara Schwartz's spirit, knowledge and wisdom lives on in the many individuals she touched throughout her career as a visionary psychologist and workshop leader. She was a pioneer in inspiring women to touch their divinity and in the way she nurtured many wounded souls back to health. Her untimely death meant that we never wrote her book; in a way, it is wrapped within these pages.

My gratitude to Stu; your patience, integrity, humor and goodness provided much needed illumination. A special word of thanks to the angelic Mari Haarldson. Hired as an assistant, you became a treasured confidante, healer and friend. Sharon Hooper, for standing at the finish line with a celestial flashlight I breathlessly thank you. I owe you a deep debt of gratitude. Fancifully brought together, you lit the tapers of patience and persistence. Your insight and guidance in the ways of the world of publishing should be a required course for inspired living. To anyone who would like to avail themselves of this lovely leader's expertise, Sharon may be reached at www.visionjourneys.com.

Friends have always been paramount in my life. I am so blessed to experience a heartfelt intensity with some very dear souls, always a sacred experience. To love, laugh and support one another in continued growth and development is essential to life itself. I acknowledge each of you deep within my being.

John, our relationship remains transcendent; the form may continue to change but the essence always endures.

Finally, the most ardent embraces to my spiritual bookends, my daughters Jenier and Alexandra. To watch each of you emerge from childhood with extraordinary integrity, character and grace has been the most awe-inspiring experience of my life. Your love and laughter continue to inspire generational healing, wonderment, continuous celebration and joy.

This book is dedicated to all of you as well as my beloved students and to all those who foster the courage to continually show up at the page.

INTRODUCTION

Your Write to Heal is a perfect companion for confronting life's hardships. Dealing with illness, confusion, financial woes, or any other of life's challenges? Looking to reinvent your self? This book will help you discover the power and support of writing as a vehicle for healing and transformation.

As defined here, healing means *coming to acceptance of what 'is' accompanied by a sense of calm knowingness.* The writing process gently leads from conflict to clarity, anxiety to peace. Emotional and mental blocks dissolve as creative energy is released. A commitment to devote time to the process described should lead to a place of increased self-knowledge and serenity.

Writing is a catalyst for connecting the conscious mind to the unconscious one where worry, fear, anxiety, and grief are stored. Often, these and other painful feelings such as resentment, jealousy and insecurity are ignored or suppressed. By developing a practice of writing as demonstrated in this book, you can become proficient at identifying certain patterns and recognizing how they may presently be sustaining pain.

Learning to write freely from the creative realm of the mind will release burdens. The writing prompts act as dams, lifting the emotional overflow up and out. The writing allows you to expose what has been buried, sometimes since early childhood. Often, just the recognition of hidden issues releases the carried load. Examples of journal entries, stories and poems by others who have used this method have been generously donated as a source of inspiration and comfort.

Discovering the immense power of free-writing was accidental for me. As a child, reading the stories of others brought solace, shielding me from life's unfair hardships. As a teen-ager, everything I consumed, from *Wuthering Heights* and *No Exit* to *Out of Africa* and anything by Colette or Tolstoy helped me develop a philosophy and sense of purpose. The joy I received through the written word made me eager to fictionalize my own experiences and reveal what I had endured. But I didn't come to the process easily, in fact the act of sitting down to write was always one of my biggest struggles.

Fear of judgment prevented me from easily expressing myself on the page. Yet I intuitively knew that writing would be my salvation. But there seemed to always be a shadowy entity hovering over me, pecking at my reluctance to face certain issues. I was being gripped by the talons of the 'writing vulture'.

Sufficiently tormented, I finally began the journey to locate my authentic self through journaling. I was a bit of a drama queen so my first year's work contained many complaints and self-pitying remarks, but what I stumbled upon by allowing myself to whine on the page uncovered most everything I needed to heal.

Since I was a teacher at the time, I began sharing what I knew about the writing process. I volunteered at Gilda's Club and witnessed transformations of the mind, soul, heart and body. I realized the immense ability for healing that people carry within themselves. I now know that there is magic in this writing process; my experience with others has shown me that this path leads to peace.

I have taught various workshops both in the U.S. and abroad, facilitating groups at various places such as The Breast Cancer Survivors' Group at Adelphi University's School for Social Research, bereavement and survivors' support groups in Europe in places as varied as Amsterdam and Venice, independent living facilities on both the east and west coasts, on-going private workshops, gang member interventions, college freshman writing classes, and high school groups for students from diverse backgrounds. I marvel as participants' insights emerge.

All I have seen affirms the enormous potential of writing. Corrective facilities are finding that writing helps inmates find a place for their rage. Medical schools teach journaling and other forms of writing as they have found that it helps doctors connect with their emotions and communicate more effectively with patients. Even institutions of higher learning such as Harvard and the University of Pennsylvania employ writing as part their curriculum on happiness.

How Does It Work?

If you keep writing—hand moving without censoring words or thoughts that arise—you are able to bypass the inner critic and jog the brain into cooperation. You can then explore the depths of your inner world, returning to the surface with new insight and wisdom. The ease of this process produces startling discoveries and makes recollections more profound.

The aim of the technique is simple, to achieve a delicate balance between staying focused and letting go. With practice, you will learn to suspend all judgment and correction. You will experience the benefit of editing at a different time, if at all. The flow is all important here. The concept might seem hard to understand, but so did learning to tie your shoes; it is in the act of doing that all is revealed.

Coming to this study, akin to perhaps yoga, prayer or meditation, forges new pathways into consciousness and creativity. There will be days when the road seems too challenging to travel. Sometimes there is confusion or despair and it seems like you are hanging on only by sheer will. Figuring out what is imperative for you at the moment (and sometimes it's just getting from one breath to the next) needs to be given validity and respect throughout your journey.

There is no one particular method for using this book (this is not school—an obvious but crucial point). Nothing is a have-to. There is no right or wrong way. You can read in a linear fashion, from cover to cover, or choose to work on whatever chapter resonates for you on that day. Explore! Do what feels right.

If possible, set aside a short block of time at least three times a week. Twenty minutes has been documented by researchers as the brain's optimum time for focusing (more about this in Chapter Two). The guided meditations in each chapter allow the mind to drift, visualize and enter a dream-like state. It is from this place that you begin to write. The exercises found in each chapter guide you in a way that gives wide berth for individual sensibilities.

The guide explains how to practice extreme care and reverence of self, so necessary while traveling this or any other road to healing. Space is given for writing short responses to particular questions; a separate journal is recommended for the actual exercises as it allows limitless space for writing.

For the sake of simplicity, the book uses the feminine perspective. While it is true that mostly women gravitate to this type of book, naturally everything within these covers is also a benefit to men.

Most of you who come to writing with trepidation find fears allayed by this method's simplicity and effectiveness. Basically, the main point is that there is no method; the challenge is to stay out of your own way. Each chapter has meditations, prompts, and affirmations.

My fervent wish is that you find guidance, motivation and inspiration within these pages. To affect change in our lives we must learn how to modify our thoughts and safely express our feelings. How we do so is what this book is about.

CHAPTER ONE:

WRITE, DON'T THINK

The Operating Manual

When going through hell, just keep going.
— Winston Churchill

Why Write?

Writing pours chatter on to the page while the heart reveals itself. Writing is about what is beneath the conscious mind. Whether you are grappling with panic, or mired in confusion, your mind can often seem to have an agenda apart from the rest of the self. It may even seem robotic since the mind repeats negative thoughts and patterns, often.

Many of us are also afflicted by worry-an exorbitant waste of energy discussed at length later in the book. To quiet mental gibberish takes intention, determination and vigilance. Only when you become aware of the self-judgments and noise can you learn to identify what the soul yearns to reveal.

Free-writing, like speaking to a best friend, can expose innermost thoughts, fears and desires. Since friends aren't always available to listen, or what you are confronting seems too much to share, learn to trust and rely on the pen to access the inner voice.

You already know how to steer a pen but self doubt is often in the rearview mirror. The skills needed to slow down and simply let your pen do the driving are discussed throughout the book. This chapter focuses on how to express from that part of you which feels safe to explore.

Writing allows the transformation of perspective, which frees you to hold thoughts and feelings with new awareness and acceptance. How you view events in life determines your sense of well-being and happiness. *Rashamon* is a famous Japanese story told from three totally different perspectives; every scene relates a different character's perception of what he or she thought had happened. The emotional impact on each creates vastly different stories.

You may see yourself as a born fighter. You may have come into the world with a strong will and lots of ambition, or you may be more vulnerable and fragile. One person's childhood may have seemed supportive, gentle and positive in outlook while another member of the same family experienced only dysfunction.

Family philosophy, environment, affiliations and peer identity all contribute to how things are now handled. The good news is that if you aren't doing as well as you'd like, though it may be challenging, you *can* change. This book will unlock the way to improving the quality of life, no matter what the situation.

PREPARING THE CANVAS

There is great value to ritualizing the process. As a prelude to actually writing you might want to sip on jasmine tea from grandmother's porcelain cup or grab a mug of joe. Part of the ritual might be to use a new, leather-bound journal for each year or issue examined, or you might prefer a yellow legal pad. Some choose fountain pens, others prefer to type. There is no one correct way, just as there is no prescribed time of day or place.

Lighting a candle hallows the space. It helps to recognize that you are worth the sacred time set aside. Time is an elusive commodity and most of us feel that we don't have any to spare. Not having free days or hours often becomes an excuse, a popular road to sabotage. The most crucial step to self-healing is to **honor the commitment to your self by carving out needed time.**

The most important ingredient is consistency of practice. *Three twenty-minute sessions is the only suggested assignment for each week* although this is not high school; there are no real requirements. Do as much or as little as feels appropriate but do note that frequent practice brings the best results. Some writers insist on writing each and every day, others write more sporadically, or only when they are with others.

I like to write while traveling, whether on a subway in New York or on a train to Giverney.

There's something about being away from my normal habitat, with all its distractions that promotes creativity and the art of observation. Maybe it is just the confinement; there is little room to wiggle and it is more conducive for focusing.

Since this doesn't occur often, I struggle to find a place and time slot that suits me. I do know that if I tell myself I will write that day I have to pretty much clear my schedule. It can take me three or four hours of wading through distractions until I can nail myself to the floor. Some writers choose to be in their beds or at the family table; others prefer libraries or the local Starbucks. I need to be tucked away in an environment with little or no distraction.

For some of you, writing with like-minded people can be a wonderfully supportive endeavor. Writing can often seem lonely and many of us are susceptible to distraction. Having someone else in the room may act as an anchor. Being in a group and reading the exercises to one another is a way to maximize the experience. Receiving positive feed-back and support is invaluable. Be willing to take the time to research this idea if it is appealing; much is written elsewhere about guidelines for starting and maintaining such groups.

Since the exercises in this book begin with closed-eye visualizations, you may want to read through the entire page first, or simply record it beforehand. The CD, with audio exercises, allows for uninterrupted participation and can be ordered through the website writerwithinworkshops.com.

Let's begin to get a feel for the process.

Exercise:

Gently close your eyes. Take a deep breath and exhale. Breathe in again and allow yourself to locate an area of stress in your body. Feel it releasing with your next exhale. Now inhale once again. Relax your shoulders as you exhale.

Softly inhale. Become aware of your thoughts and feelings floating by but do not attach to any one of them. Gently exhale. Watch a thought go by and comment "Isn't that interesting?" Be aware of yourself in a place of neutrality. Feel yourself settling down into your body. Inhale deeply and imagine digging your feet into soil or sand. Exhale and experience the earth; feel supported and rooted. This is known as *grounding*.

Now, take a deep breath and think of one thing you wish to change. Let it be something that is either bringing you pain or preventing you from feeling at peace. Take a few deep breaths as you bring something to mind. It can be something about yourself or a situation. Gently release your breath.

What is it you would like to manifest? Is it something within your power to obtain? Or, is it something which cannot be changed but calls for acceptance? Identify and release one thing that hinders your progress. Inhale. Visualize your breath entering and surrounding your heart, providing support. Exhale.

Come slowly back into the room and begin to write about what came to mind. How does it make you feel? Remember to write without pausing. Practice training your mind to ignore judgmental comments or messages about spelling and punctuation by just noticing when you chastise yourself. Gently let the thoughts go without beating yourself up for having them. Erase intrusive ideas or reminders about picking things up at the cleaner's or watering the philodendron. Just keep the pen moving and watch the words flow on to the page.

After you have written for twenty minutes, sit back and let whatever emotions surface to just be; if you find tears appearing, let them flow. If you wish to, reread what you have written but know that many writers choose to let the material just sit unread for a day, a week or forever. It is the act of writing, more than *what* you have written, that heals.

You might want to keep note of how you felt as you were writing and record how emotions are experienced as the day progresses; become aware of your activity level and eating habits, whether or not you interact with others during the day and how you sleep that night.

Remember to let your mind wander in these exercises. If any exercise does not suggest something to you either let it go and write about whatever does come up, including any resistance or dislike of the prompt. There is no correct subject you must write on; listen to your inner voice.

Have compassion for the little child you were, the one who might have felt unsafe and puzzled. Know that you may be experiencing these familiar feelings now as they often are triggered by stress, illness, grief, or anxiety.

Ask Yourself:

Did I have the power to change anything in my past?

____

____

Am I remembering childhood wounds differently than the way they actually happened? What do I see now as an adult that is different than the way I have been holding the memory? Am I still powerless?

____

____

____

You have the opportunity to shower yourself with feelings of being protected, loved and accepted, now. This isn't a quick-fix procedure; it is a process of becoming aware of the negative and stopping the thought or emotion without feeling guilt. Try to replace the negative thoughts, words and patterns with gentle, positive wording. Doing this while going through a crisis may seem monumental but then, how many of us work at changing when things are going well?

Can you look with an adult's detachment at a father's alcoholism, a mother's early death, a brother's abuse? Can you then release the crushing effect it might have had on you when you were a child? If nothing comes to mind regarding an unsafe feeling from childhood consider yourself blessed and ask what did frighten or threaten you. Perhaps it was something small in retrospect (a fear of dogs, spiders or your cousin's friend) but try to recall how it loomed before you then.

Find a quiet place within yourself now, in this present moment. Do not think about what may come, just luxuriate in the breath; you are here now, protected. At this moment you are safe.

In the next twenty minutes allow yourself to describe the incident or situation from your past. Describe the wounds and the scars. Honor your bravery the way you would pay homage to any other heroine. Be kind, compassionate and celebratory. Reward the person you have become with praise.

Karla comes to the workshop I facilitate at Gilda's Club. She had been diagnosed with Hodgkin's Disease while in college, yet after five years she was given a clean bill of health. When her illness reappeared thirty years later she was blindsided. Some days she valiantly walks in with her faith intact. At other times her humanness, her fragility is apparent. Throughout it all she is gentle, intelligent and present:

> *On the way today, I was thinking about how tired I felt. It reminded me of when I was sick and really couldn't get around much. I used to look out the window and see people walking, window-shopping, pushing babies in prams, walking their dogs, having lunch in the outdoor cafes. I so wanted to be out with them. And this would happen day after day. I never felt better overnight. In a month or sometimes a week, energy would come or discomfort would recede—a little, no tangible progress, just little atoms of better, but nothing to get excited about.*
>
> *...there were times when I wished to die—the thought of continuing as it was seemed unbearable. There was a block of lovely carving knives in the kitchen and lots of meds in the house. Too many beta-blockers or Ambiens would pretty much do the job.*
>
> *But—the knives would hurt, and after I took the pills, I couldn't get them back—and worst of all—I'm Catholic—suicide is a mortal sin—and I'd burn, baby burn! I've spent too much time trying to be good to blow it.*
>
> *So I'd summon up my life experiences and my inner Scarlett O'Hara and write, "Karla, tomorrow will be a better day." Well, not necessarily this tomorrow, but on one of the tomorrows one of these days and with a good dose of patience I'd get there. A week or a month would go by and as miserable as I was, I'd keep writing and I'd feel stronger and better.*

Have you been viewing a current situation with old, worn-out worries and fears? Can you see an ancient betrayal as another person's defect instead of as personal rejection?

Memories from childhood hold many answers but they only hurt if given permission. Here, in the present moment, is where the real energy lies. Here in the present moment you are a sage. Like cleaning out a childhood room, writing about people, places and events allows you to keep the treasures and restore or discard those harmful or limiting memories.

Exorcising through writing, which is necessary when painful recollections seem like stubborn demons, can bring back the experience in reframed, healthy ways. It may also bring up some strong, uncomfortable energy. Mostly, however, it allows inner wisdom to surface, opening the heart to what actually is, as opposed to what isn't. Writing permits you to make amends, declare your new wishes and release outworn patterns or toxic thoughts. Writing encourages the creation of new programming.

Sarah was the daughter of two Holocaust survivors. She was stifled by her mother's constant worrying and being over-protective.

> *I was always getting into trouble. I rebelled in any way that I knew how. The first time I wrote about how I hated my mother and how she stunted me. The next few times I told myself that I was willing to look at things from her side. One day I wrote in her voice and the picture-window in my head shattered. It was as powerful as anything I had read or seen in a movie. I was suddenly transported back in time and viscerally felt the fear my mother had felt.*
>
> *By allowing myself to write, without restriction, I experienced the fright coursing through my veins. I realized that I probably did carry her on a cellular level and that I had wanted to get away from her my whole life. I'd like to say that I healed my relationship with her that day but it wasn't so. It took two more years of writing twice a week-once in a therapist's office-until I was able to forgive what had been done to me. My mother is an old woman now. I have learned to heal myself of regret and to honor and comfort her the best way I know how. I am more present than ever; I give of myself freely having broken the chains that had bound us both. I remind myself every morning and every night that I am grateful to my mother for fighting, not only for her own survival...but also for mine.*

It is important to stay **vigilant** to new programming. The old ways are forever lying in wait to take control and have us stuck in distress again. All we need is the **willingness** (as used for this purpose: *focused energy sent in the direction of one's intention*) to heal. We must relax and be open to having faith in our wisdom, then the answers we are seeking will manifest.

There is a second part to this simple process:

While writing freely we need to remind ourselves to accept what is happening and to be conscious that our understanding of it might be limited in the moment. Then we need to take the time allotted for reflection and affirmation. This is essential to self-growth.

Affirmations are succinct statements of wisdom that are repeated over and over to implement change. *If you eliminate this step, your old or unhealthy patterns are apt to re-emerge.* **There is an affirmation at the end of each chapter in this book. You may also want to create your own. Check and make sure that the messages you tell yourself are entirely positive.**

Sometimes you may come to the page to express feelings of weakness or self pity. Do not judge this harshly. Seeing stored-up thoughts and feelings on paper allows them to be viewed objectively and an attitude of extreme care for your young self to be considered. In our society extreme self care is often considered selfish, indulgent or frivolous and is frequently confused with vanity. Be strong and know that it is not so.

The reality is that women are now experiencing heart attacks and other stress-related ailments at a previously unknown rate. It is crucial to realize that you must care for your self, otherwise you cannot be available to nurture others effectively. What is extreme self care? It is such an essential component to healing that a whole chapter is devoted to it (please see Chapter Five).

Take a moment to list some of the ways you *do* nurture yourself such as setting aside time to walk each day either alone or with a friend. Thoreau wrote that he was able to walk away from any problem he ever had, no matter how daunting.

No need to feel obligated to fill each space—take your own approach to this exercise. You may want to add to this list each time you develop another way of nurturing yourself:

1. ______________________________
____

2. ______________________________
____

3. ______________________________
____

4. ______________________________
____

5. ______________________________
____

6. ______________________________
____

7. ______________________________
____

8. ______________________________
____

9. ______________________________
____

10. ______________________________
____

Now list a number of ways that you *don't* take care of yourself, such as emotional eating, lack of sleep, or not allowing time for fun.

1. ______________________________

2. ______________________________

3. ______________________________

4. ______________________________

5. ______________________________

6. ______________________________

7. ______________________________

8. ______________________________

9. ______________________________

10. ______________________________

Always look for the *feeling* that you are trying to mask or suppress in regard to these thoughts or behaviors. Know that expressing gratitude and appreciation for what you do for yourself leads to a sense of sublime well-being and produces the motivation to continue. Be open to having faith that when falling off the 'program' you will come back stronger the next day. Babies didn't learn to be toddlers by giving up. Crawl, or try to stand; practice with determination and love!

Embrace the gift of self nourishment by starting each day with some quick, inspirational reading such as Sarah Ban Breathnach's **Simple Abundance: A Daybook of Comfort and Joy**, (Warner Books, 2009) or read a meditation from **Meditations For Women Who Do Too Much**, (Harper & Row, 2008) by Anne Wilson Schaef.

Write, don't think. What does that truly mean? Writing as an extension of the heart while keeping the mind still means that you can release all that has been suppressed.

Writing nonstop for twenty minutes allows your authentic voice to emerge, releasing blocked energy. Besides moving the pen and just writing what surfaces—no matter how disjointed it may seem, ask the chattering mind and the inner critic to be quiet for now.

Here's an example written in twenty minutes by Josie on an average day while recovering from a double mastectomy.

> *I can't stand to look at myself today. Yesterday was better; how long will this go on? I can't stand the way Sean fawns all over me. If I wanted to get out of this relationship before I want to twice as much now. But who will have me—who wants damaged goods? Who will look at me, ever again? I am at the effect of other people's glances. Does everyone know? I am worthless. Really? Listen to yourself! You should be ashamed. Stop…who is this-my mother? The nuns? I know better, my brain knows better-I am a high school principal for God's sake. I need to soothe myself. I need to forgive myself. I am more than my wounds, I am more than my experiences. I am valiant. I have come through this and I will take on whatever comes my way. I will never ask "Why me?" again. I am so ungrateful. Stop-there I go again. I am human. I am hurt. I am scared. I*

> *deserve compassion. I give it to everyone else. I am remembering to give it to me now. I can acknowledge all the love and support I get without staying in a dead-end relationship. I can acknowledge Sean. I still have plenty of life in me. I am still attractive. I still have worth. I can give love and I am ready to receive some, also.*

Twenty minutes is not an arbitrary time period, but grounded in research on how the brain works. Studies have shown that this time is optimum for focused concentration. Know that with practice, pens begin to flow with greater ease. This may be challenging at first, yet a conscious effort to keep the pen in motion will pay off.

What if you hit a snag? Just keep writing the last word recorded, over and over and something will catch, just as jumper cables help restart a stalled car's motor.

Beware of the Inner Critic! Who? Most of us have something in our heads which is constantly judging, correcting or berating. This is more highly developed in those of us who came from critical or rigid homes.

When this voice speaks, you do not want to get rid of it completely as it often keeps you from harm, helps you refine or edit, and goads you on to ever higher achievement. However, this is the voice that needs to be tamed, or caged, at times. It has no place when you need to be "out of your mind" with creativity. If you quiet the mind your heart and soul can be heard. Befriend your brain, even though it sometimes seems tyrannical. Reassure that part of you just as a parent calms an unruly child; you do not want to obliterate it but teach your little tyrant the proper place in your life.

All of this work requires new behaviors and habits which can be learned at any age. I often hear from my students that all this is *hard*; I ask that we substitute the word *challenging*. It has an entirely different connotation and quality. **When you are faced with something challenging, you know there is a solution and your natural fighter kicks in. You become hopeful while forging uncharted pathways.**

Scientists have also discovered that the brain develops new neural pathways each time it learns something, even at age ninety. You can definitely change your thinking which does change the way you feel about things; this is an extreme challenge! You must have the intention to fulfill your desire for peace of mind. The strength of such intention will carry the burden of repetition and be on the alert when the old patterns reemerge (and they do—constantly) until you are able to manifest the desired results.

Through the practice of writing you can learn to visualize your inner world as a smooth and flowing entity. I used to experience my emotions so intensely, with such attachment; it was as if my innards were lined with Velcro. I felt my sadness or frustration and dragged it along like Sarah Bernhardt, my vision of an emotional bag lady. I was so weighed down with life's Sturm und Drang that I avoided confronting anything additional. I was exhausted (and exhausting). Through writing I learned how to feel without attaching to the emotions. I am able to do this often now, but definitely not all the time. I still have to remind myself, or someone will surely tell me. It is liberating to observe and release what had previously been scary or painful. Tremendous energy is released and additional internal space is made available.

You are able to handle anything in your life if you have a purpose. If it is to assist yourself and others, know that you must learn how to release the past and come into each present moment where you are always safe.

"What is healing but a shift in perspective?" poet Mark Doty asks. Many authors say that without writing, life would not be worth living. It provides them with purpose and meaning. Articulate *your* purpose. If you are not in touch with what this may be, now is the time to find out.

What if you loosened the heaped dirt that has accumulated over your lifetime? It falls away in the time that it takes to realize that the past no longer has any power. Step into the present and grab what is real and vibrant now, in this-the only-moment.

Exercise:

Close your eyes. Take a deep breath, listening to the sound your intake of air makes. Exhale all the air from your lungs, experiencing the release of tension.

Picture yourself being carried along a quiet, flowing river. You are gently floating, unaffected by any thing or anyone. Inhale deeply, imagining clean, clear air enveloping you as snuggly as an infant's bunting. Breathe as you pass by old mistakes, pains and loss. Watch as they disappear over the falls. You see everything but none of it has any effect. You are totally detached. Imagine releasing toxins and stuck energy into the river. The water renders them inert. As they leave they evaporate; you are being cleansed. Breathe in…exhale.

Take a breath through your nose, picturing the air traveling to your heart, gently caressing and bringing comfort. Exhale and release any grief, or sadness that may present itself, either through memories or waves of emotion. Cry or sigh deeply. Breathe in...exhale.

Inhale gently and deeply exhale either through your mouth, or nose, whichever is more comfortable. The breaths should be deep, audible and even. The rhythm of this is calming and helps keep you in a meditative state. Relax for a few moments.

It's time now to leave the river behind and step out on to the riverbank. Plant yourself where you can observe your world with loving detachment. Imagine roots growing from the bottoms of your feet, unfurling into the rich, loamy, regenerative soil. You are grounded and supported. Breathe in ...exhale.

Inhale and visualize the energy coming in through your roots, coursing throughout your body. Exhale. Inhale once more and imagine the breath swirling around your pelvic region, the center of power. Visualize the breath sweeping the area of past trauma and disappointment. Remember: only that which you feel safe to let go of will detach. Release.

Inhale once more. Guide the breath up to your head, aware of negative or judgmental thoughts residing there. You may come across memories or visuals of parents, teachers and other authorities. Know that they no longer need to negatively influence your actions or choices.

Now visualize yourself before puberty. The revered novelist Willa Cather said that everything an author needs to write about happened before the age of twelve. See your inner child as she once was. If you have difficulty conjuring up a visual, locate a photo from that time in your mind's eye. When you have this child, allow a memory of something which occurred at that time when you were *not* honored, and your true self was not allowed to surface. Find as many details as you can such as people's tones of voice, their demeanor and body language. Where were they looking as they spoke to you? Were they supportive? Intimidating? Were you lonely? Filled with shame or anger?

When you have finished, open your eyes partially, focusing only on the paper as you put this book down. Pick up your pen. It is now time to write. Describe, in as much detail as you can, one person you encountered during the meditation. How did he, or she, dishonor you? Were you bullied, not believed, treated coldly or abused? Keep the pen moving, letting the images surface without any judgment.

It might not be immediately apparent why a particular thought surfaces. Trust that it will come to you at a later time. Keep the pen moving for the full twenty minutes.

What conversations took place at that time? Write, without thinking, without stopping. If you can't remember something, invent it; memory and imagination come from the same area in the brain. Your imagination will start connecting with the memory of what actually occurred. If you find yourself going into another topic, allow that. It may lead you somewhere. At any time, with these experiences, if you find that it is too painful to write about the topic, write about the fear, the pain, about how it can only touch you now if you allow it to. Breathe with this. Now put the pen down.

Inhale…exhale. Read what you have written. It is common for us to have adult insight and wisdom emerge that we had not been aware of before. Sit quietly, allowing thoughts and feelings to flow and the emotional responses that surface to just be present. You may want to write about these also. Connections to your present situation may continue to materialize, often at random times. Are you holding the memories with a child's eye, retaining a child's hurt? If so, take the time now to reframe the incident as an adult, with a mature, compassionate perspective.

Honor the child and what she was feeling at the time of the incident you remember. Perhaps the reasons you were singled out or bullied had nothing to do with you. Maybe your mother really loved you but was disconnected from everyone, not just you. Perhaps she didn't know how to express her affection, for reasons unknown. Honor the child and what she was feeling at the time. Acknowledge the pain and comfort her with present awareness. Know that this reclaimed memory is affecting your beliefs and attitudes today. Be willing to let the feelings go and just keep the lesson.

As Buddha knew thousands of years ago, when we stay in the present moment, all is well. We are safe. It is when we return to the past or jump into what might happen in the future that we falter. Negative messages take us out of the present. They keep us in resentment, regret and misery. Affirmations bring us back to the present.

Whatever you are confronting can be handled with a strong core. Think of a willow tree. It may bend in the wind until an observer is sure that it will snap…but it doesn't. It eventually recovers and straightens once more. Writing shows that you are like the willow; become aware of your flexibility and strength.

Through writing we explore how to hold ourselves in the present moment. It is where we are safe. It is where Eastern religion and philosophy state that there is peace. Those who meditate, pray or practice yoga can attest to this. The quality of our lives increases exponentially; we get to see the other parts of ourselves usually lost in the fog of stress or pain. We discover why we withhold from ourselves.

Tell yourself: even though I have been wronged, there is no need to continue to wrong myself. I am willing to forgive and let the pain go, lighten up, and release. It is time to let it go. The past no longer controls me. I am safe in the present moment.

If you are willing to say these statements out loud, it increases the effect of change exponentially. Kristen, a student who has been attending class for a few years wrote, "When someone told me to let go I instinctively clutched tighter than ever. Why? I didn't trust. I was taught to expect that the worst would happen. It took me an entire adult year to stop listening to that voice and to catch myself every time I had to confront something that *could* go wrong. I now remind myself how much good is really in my life, how many good things (constantly) do happen."

The old mind is strong and it has a lot invested in staying put. The ego, where these messages reside, fears giving up control to our authentic selves. The ego is fearful, the authentic self is ever-patient and loving. We need to flood the ego with goodness in order to disarm it. This requires dedication and repetition.

Write the affirmations at the end of each chapter on index cards and carry them with you, saying them often. Leave them placed around your environment where you'll see them. Put them in a drawer, on your night table, on the bathroom mirror, the car's dashboard, even the refrigerator. This is an integral step in developing healthier self-talk. Many books and CD's are available regarding affirmations. Anything by Louise Hay is recommended.

Now allow yourself to visually rake the nostalgia or melancholy away.

Ask:

Who am I without all these sickeningly sweet, familiar memories?
How can I reframe my story in a healthy way?

Answer:

Exercise:

Go into a relaxed state, as before. In your mind's eye see something or someone dear to you (know that they do not have to be living at present). Imagine everything that made it special to be in the presence of who or what fills you with awe. Utilizing all of your five senses, visualize a loving encounter.

When you have the vision and are ready, come back into the room. Without being distracted by what is going on around you, pick up the pen. Imagine that the pen is an extension of your mind and heart. Describe in detail what you have just witnessed. What feelings were you accessing? Now express thoughts and feelings about what you have envisioned. Let your pen wander. This may lead to somewhere more profound than you actually imagined. Keep the critical voice at bay anytime it surfaces.

After the full twenty minutes of writing without pausing (except, perhaps to shake your hand out) place the pen down and take a few deep breaths. It is fine to decide to leave and return to read this later. Permit the flow of whatever needs to come up and out. Feel the increased space within.

Acknowledge the person and your relationship without him or her, in writing. Even if you are no longer in communication with this person, know that he or she will always be part of your story.

Now rest.

Everyone's life is worth a novel.
-Gustav Flaubert

AFFIRMATIONS:

I welcome safety and wisdom in this moment. The only reality I accept is in the present. (Breathe).

It is safe for me to release my attachment to the past. I am learning to be in this moment. This is my only reality.

Summary:

- Write, don't think; let the thoughts surface on the page naturally.
- Free-writing allows access to innermost thoughts, fears and desires.
- Ritualizing the process and maintaining consistency of practice establishes new healthy habits.
- Honoring the commitment to self-healing by carving out needed time is imperative.
- Becoming aware of and quieting the inner critic allows for non-judgment in writing and other areas.

CHAPTER TWO:

RELEASING THE SAFETY VALVE

The Transformation of Wounds

All sorrows can be borne, if you put them into a story.
— Isak Dinesen

We each have levers to release sorrow, anger, and regret, crucial components of the healing process. Just as old-time radiators have valves which control the amount of steam released at any given time, if emotions build up inside and are not released, we explode. Writing is an optimally functioning release system.

Losses and how they are dealt with can be a governing part of life's journey. Basic nature coupled with family custom creates healthy behavioral patterns; dysfunctional attitudes and coping mechanisms can be crippling. However, there is no need to stay stuck.

Eleanor, brilliant and accomplished, traveled around the world lecturing on the applications of nuclear medicine. While at a conference in Sweden she felt a lump in her breast and took herself to the office of a world renowned doctor. Without telling her family and friends why Eleanor extended her stay for two additional months. She underwent chemotherapy in Geneva, refusing to discuss the matter with anyone, even her husband. This stoic woman was compliant with her doctor's orders and had regular six month check-ups upon returning home, always receiving a report of good health. As the five year mark came to a close, the local internist found a tumor in her other breast.
This time, after much inner searching, she decided to have a double mastectomy and reconstructive surgery. Her doctor recommended that she attend my workshops as part of the process. At first, she had to force herself to write. Stored-up terror began to surface as she developed courage. Eleanor came from an accomplished family that faced life head-on and dealt with challenges promptly. She acknowledged always feeling different than the rest of her siblings—they never discussed emotions. Now she allowed herself to cry, rant and rage on to the page, uncovering a well of strength beneath her fear.

"I sit here in this class and listen to how others had to battle without reserves of love and support. Believe it or not, this has given me the extra strength I need to go on. I have been humbled by the others. I now realize what real courage is, and I want it."

She went on, "Releasing all this pent-up anguish and anger is keeping me from collapsing or making myself sicker. What I have discovered from writing about my past is the reason why I have found it difficult to be open. I was never allowed to talk about my feelings as a child. I had strong emotions but couldn't express them. Now I feel able to talk about anything to my husband and grown children."

"I know that I have made the right decision because I am now at peace," she shared with the group, "I want to live. I live to work. I'm fifty six years old and have raised my family. I don't want to be haunted by disease anymore. I wasn't ready to confront this before and lived in constant fear that the cancer would return. Now that it has, I am taking control of my relationship with myself and others. I guess that is the gift from all of this. This is what is going to last forever."

Ruth first came to class at Gilda's Club about a year after her husband passed away. She had been an avid music fan during her teen years in Beatle dominated England. "Writing in rhymed couplet brings clarity and comfort," she told us; "it speeds the letting go of anger and rage, replacing it with something of beauty."

"I never wrote poetry before coming to this group. I always remembered the rhythm and lyrics of songs but I honestly don't know where these words are coming from now. I attended a bereavement group right after Eric died, and that helped but nothing compares to turning all of this energy into something creative. I don't know how I do it but I do know why."

Ruth has been coming to class practically every week for the last seven years. She is a wonder; no matter what the exercise or prompt, she is able to produce exquisite, meaningful poetry. A teacher of yoga, she knows how to get out of her own way. She shows up at the page and weaves what has been on her mind and in her heart that week. She allows a half hour before class to go down to the shore in my town. "I just sit by the water and let nature have her way with me. I am calmed and soothed, then ready to write. I come to class because it is a refuge. I honestly don't know what I would do with all my unnamed feelings during this time if I weren't channeling them like this."

Courage…faith…determination…patience. We all possess certain strengths, even though our awareness of what they may be is not always so easily accessed.

I WRITE BECAUSE ....

I write to heal myself and thus to figure out
Who I am and why I'm here
What life is all about

I explore my limitations
Open up my inner soul
Expose the imperfections
In the hopes I'll end up whole

I write about my past
My childhood and my home
I remember all the heartaches
How it was to feel alone

I write of inspirations
That I found along the way
Of people who have touched me
By what they do or what they say

I write to capture moments
Which are etched upon my mind
So they won't be lost forever
In the floods of passing time

I write to remember people
And adventures that have passed
So that lives can make a difference
When they disappear so fast

I write to grieve my husband
For the years we did not share
I write to thank my parents
For their love and for their care

I write to help humanity
Understand just who we are
So somehow we'll save the Planet
Before we view it from afar

I write to open doorways
Into my mind and to my heart
So I can express my deepest longings
And in this Play to do my part

I write to find my purpose
To discover why I'm here
I write to seek my passion
And to overcome my fear

I write to heal my body
To soothe my spirit and my mind
And unearth my wildest fantasies
Leave limitations far behind

I write for what is possible
For the miracles in life
To maximize potential
Walk the sharp blade of the knife

I write to justify being
A contribution to this world
To record the path I'm walking
As my journey has unfurled

I write to honor teachers
Whose wisdom I have sought
Their inspiration lives inside me
It's not something that was taught

But rather it's a feeling
An awareness passed along
By simply being in their presence
Or in their words, or in a song

For we never know the impact
A simple word or glance can give
An energy transformation
To a better way to live

So where's my writing going
I'm not sure and so I'll trust
That it's beyond my comprehension
Perhaps it's scattered like the dust

It's given back to those who'll listen
To pass along for ears to hear
And if it never leaves these pages
Then the purpose will be clear

It's for my very own salvation
For my ears only without force
So I can find my destination
To return me to my Source

Although I'd like to honor others
All those who offered me a hand
When I was in my darkest canyons
They helped me understand

That this is just an opportunity
To live each moment, day by day
And expressing it in writing
Has been my chosen way

Ruth T. Netter

EXERCISE:

Allow your feet to be firmly planted, uncrossed, on the floor. Close your eyes and breathe deeply through your nose. Let yourself settle into the breath–this time becoming aware of the air as it travels to your throat, the center of expression. Swirl it around, collecting blockages, negative, unproductive thoughts and unexpressed emotions. Release as much of the toxin as possible.

Breathe in deeply as the breath goes down to your shoulders; feel it cloaking you in comfort. Exhale with an audible sigh. Inhale and let the air unknot any held stress and emotion. Gently breathe out.

Now, on the inhale, feel the air reaching down to your heart as the breath clears some aches, lost hopes and unaddressed losses.

Breathe, allowing the air to gather some of what you no longer need.

Allow yourself to sit with a feeling of emptiness, of stillness. This may feel uncomfortable, or bring up strong emotions. View whatever arises from a detached vantage point. You can feel the emotions and watch them as they rise up then drift away.

When you are ready, identify one disappointment in your life that has had a profound effect on you. Spend a few moments allowing thoughts to rise to your consciousness. Observe and be aware of *unbidden memories* coming to mind. If no recollection comes, permit whatever you are seeing within to surface.

Watch your thoughts flow, and when ready, slowly open your eyes and begin to write about the experience. For the next twenty minutes put your feelings into words. You may want to start by describing what you saw, what you remember. It may have nothing to do with what you *thought* would appear.

Remember that we should not try to control what comes up. There is no right or wrong image. As this type of writing accesses the unconscious mind, any memory or topic can be a catalyst to finding a cause of your pain (or forgotten joy). Ask if you are able, or ready, to view this experience with detachment.

Be still for a while. Read what you just wrote and remind yourself that this all comes from the past and that it no longer has to have a profound hold on life today. Be alert to your thinking, to the power assigned to the past. Watch as insights appear. Strengthen the commitment to having compassion for yourself and for who you once were.

It's not uncommon to feel emptied out after writing but remember that you are safe. You may even want to take a nap. Be receptive and listen to your body's needs.

One of my students, a professional musician, had a son who was away at college. He called her one morning, complaining of chest pains. She advised him to go to the hospital and call her as soon as possible. An hour or two later the emergency room doctor called to say that Tyler had returned to the hospital. He hadn't been able to breathe but now was resting. They didn't know the cause of the distress but would keep in touch as they planned to keep him overnight for observation. They assured Paula and her husband that there was no need for concern and no need to make the drive. Later that day, the school's doctor called asking if she and her husband could come right away. By the time they arrived after the four hour drive, their son had passed away. Over the next year she dealt with the shock and pain trying various ways, most successfully by playing the viola. This was her natural outlet. But she still found that she couldn't face the depth of grief until she started to write.

"At first, I wrote about the need for sleep and escape. I found words and images coming to me; they either brought me solace or they wracked me with grief and I just couldn't write until I had cried to release some. Then, as soon as I wrote, I felt at peace. Over the following months I returned and reread what I had written. I began formulating the random thoughts into poems."

She collected them into a book which she self-published and has shared with many others who needed the comfort. However, her husband and other son did not have either the gift or the tools for expressing themselves, and struggled. They told her that they were afraid of forgetting. Her husband said that not enough time had passed for him to feel better.

Recovering does not mean letting go of the loved one. It means releasing the pain and retaining the love; it means getting back to life. Many who are mourning, ill, or challenged become consumed by their condition. It is reasonable and normal to feel this way for a while, but then we must find a way to move on, to realize that we are so much more than any disease, loss or problem. Many of us find this event or condition dominating our entire lives. In order to feel better we must be *willing* to release the reservoir of sadness.

How? With awareness. This may sound oversimplified but without it you cannot deal with anything, let alone a life-altering situation. Later in the book I discuss the best way to release a stuck habit. Harsh as it may sound, extended mourning, or being at the effect of an illness or divorce, is actually another form of habit. Religion, literature, philosophy and science, all address this issue. If you are suffering, get in touch with your feelings of attachment through daily writing and make a commitment to emerge from the pain. Watch the feelings without judgment as they rise before you; bless them as the hurt washes away. Remember that your experience of the beloved does not fade only the pain associated with the loss does.

Legend has it that there was an old man whose wife died early one morning. Later that night he was seen dancing in the village square. Horrified, the villagers asked him why he wasn't home, mourning. He told them, "I know that I have to accept this and move on sooner or later. I'm just choosing sooner."

Zorba the Greek, one of literature's great characters, told his neighbors on the island that he was embracing the "whole catastrophe" of life when his wife died. He also lost all his possessions, yet was able to find peace and joy, no matter what.

Most of us are not brought up on small islands or are Zen Buddhists. We must be honest enough to examine why we remain sad or miserable for an extended time instead of rejoining life. I have found myself wanting to climb up and out, or pass through, a state of mourning but have not been able to budge. There was a natural comfort in mourning and a fear of what was to be if I let go.

Let writing be your guide for reaching awareness and resolution.

An endearing student of mine experienced something profound when she tried this for the first time. Vivacious and erudite she called herself a neophyte as a writer. She first started coming to class to write her memoirs for her grown children and their families. Her childhood had been quite intense and she wrote stories that she had never shared with anyone before. She certainly didn't come to the workshops to heal anything (these were my Writer Within classes for creative writing) and she did not particularly see herself as a writer.

She had been a widow for ten years and was just starting to date. She had just recently met a gentleman who caught her fancy. He was attentive but she sensed that he wasn't ready for a relationship, having been widowed for just a year and a half. She experienced anxiety each time she was about to see him.

"I feel like a sixteen year old," she told me.

One Friday night I happened to speak to her on the phone and she confided, "I was so anxious last night I hardly slept." We discussed all the reasons for her upset yet she couldn't shake the feeling. "You need to let the anxiety speak to you. It obviously wants to tell you something. Go have a dialogue, a written conversation with the discomfort and let it communicate what it will," I suggested.

She promised that she would and called the next morning, astonished. "I wrote and wrote and wrote. The writing took me back to my childhood and the punishment I always suffered each time I expressed myself. I can see now that I am so afraid of expressing all the love I have to give and am afraid that I will once again be locked away in my room." She realized that her fear about dating this man had nothing to do with whether he liked her, or was ready for a relationship.

She was incredulous that the out-of-mind writing brought back the corridors of her unconscious to the childhood room and punishment she received whenever she expressed feelings or said what was on her mind. She shared how the experience opened a floodgate of painful memories about being ignored and made to feel invisible. "When my husband died I must have viewed losing my true love as punishment. I guess that I've been afraid that if I feel once more I will be locked away, forever."

"Are you still feeling any of the anxiety?" I queried. "No, none at all," she replied, surprised.

DIALOGUING EXERCISE:

Come to a place of relaxed breathing with a few inhales, reciting the Sanskrit meditative sound *'So'* and a few exhales to the sound *'Hum'* until you feel yourself conscious of energy coursing through your veins, arteries and bones. Imagine this force traveling from the base of your spine, through the top of your head, continuing up into the ethers, where -it branches out as a golden antenna, gathering light and power. Connect with this wisdom as it is conducted back into your being in the form of liquid gold. Exhale.

Now allow yourself to identify an unpleasant physical sensation, an emotional pain, a fear or chronic complaint.Visualize what this *thing* looks like. Is it a smelly, gaseous material? A fiery or foggy substance?

Ask it what it wants, why it won't leave you, what its message is. Allow it to tell you why it first appeared. What would you have to do to make it disappear? How can you make peace and thank it for guiding, or perhaps even protecting you?

This form of dialoguing is a very powerful tool. Use it often. Much of the research done on this and other forms of writing with patients in hospitals and rehab facilities has shown that participants show fewer symptoms of illness than those who do not practice writing!

Memoir is one of the workshops I teach at a resort-like independent living facility. I have a wonderful core group of gentlewomen from whom I learn a lot. I try to focus on positive memories with them and am in awe of the courage they display when they access something painful.

One day the exercise involved music. Students were asked to recall a specific concert, composer or experience that revealed the role music had played in their lives. Edith read what she had written with a quavering voice.When she was done she looked up as the light caught the glistening of her moist eyes.

> *There was always music playing in our house. My husband would come home from work and twirl me in time with whatever the radio or stereo was playing. After he died I never turned on either again. I couldn't bear it. One day my daughter came to visit and without thinking she just turned on the radio. Automatically I demanded that she turn it off. As I write today*

> *I realize that by not listening, I was keeping myself in a state of mourning, I was denying the memories of how happy and joyful we had been. This is how I am healing, I thought I was through mourning, but I'm obviously not. I don't know why I'm crying now. I'm not sure if it's from missing Harry, reliving those wonderful memories, or for having denied my daughter pleasure during those years following his death. I just know that I'm going to keep writing it all down: the joy, the pain, and now, finally, the relief.*

Debbie Ford (www.DebbieFord.com) leads workshops based on the concept of our shadow, the parts of ourselves that we fail to love. By embracing both the good and the bad we learn that we are complete. If we're truly honest we will discover that there have been secret payoffs to staying stuck, to being a victim. When we get to a point where we have been emptied out, we realize that those prior beliefs and roles do not support who we really are.

Ask:

When do I feel like a victim?

____

____

Where did I feel like a victim earlier in my life?

____

____

There has been much written in other sources about victimhood and guilt, most notably **Goodbye to Guilt** by Gerald Jampolsky (New York: Bantam Books, 2009) and **Healing the Shame that Binds Us** by John Bradshaw (Deerfield Beach: Health Communications, Inc., 2007). The bottom line is that if you feel like a victim you don't have to take responsibility. This may sound extremely harsh, yet it is meant to be a gentle wake-up call. You've done the best you could with the information you had. When you come to realize that you have control, not over what happens but how you deal with it, you can have peace.

In my Thursday writing class, Helene was moaning about her deceased lover and how insensitive that partner's family had been to her. Helene and Mark lived together for years and she dutifully, lovingly, took care of him when he became terminally ill. His family had never really accepted her and the fact that the couple had chosen not to marry. When he was hospitalized, his relatives did their best to show up and help. Helene was suddenly called away on urgent business and Mark sank into a coma. His brother and sister-in-law promised that they would keep him on life support until she got back. They then made the decision to let him go without informing her. This had occurred over four years before she started attending the workshops. Every week she wrote out the same story and remained in the same place. Finally she saw what she was doing when she realized that she had filled a notebook with complaints and laments but no growth. She then developed her intention to move on.

It is perplexing how mourning a loved one or feeling afraid of illness and loss can be described as "being stuck". Refer back to the first chapter where feeling emotions without attaching to them is discussed. Remaining in the same place for extended periods of time can be considered stagnation. It is understandable considering the depth of grief; the fear of losing all connection to the person by letting go of the pain is something that is often written about in class.

Nowhere in her writing had Helene been letting go and getting under the story. By staying attached to the facts, she remained in her role of the victim. If she were to let her *self* speak, she would have to move on and then who would she be? Who would she be without her story? By slowly, carefully, allowing herself to answer those questions, she healed, while retaining the beautiful yet tragic memory. She had been afraid of being invisible without her partner and without the drama. She released the pent-up guilt and blame, wrote letters to his family (she never mailed them) and forgave herself for having been away. She was able to garner strength, access her innate wisdom and move on, knowing that she had been loved.

Telling stories with intention can create new meaning and purpose in your life. I feel that if I can retell my story in a way that helps others, then I halve the grief I have suffered and hopefully lessen theirs, also.

Your intention may be to release depression, obsessive thoughts, or irresponsible actions. Stating an intention is like pulling the chord to raise the curtain which has been cloaking clarity; it galvanizes your inner resources and aligns them with the energy needed for change.

A young woman who attended my workshops at Gilda's Club came with the intention to capture memories of her mother who had passed away after a long battle with cancer. She wanted to retain the memory of her mother as a healthy, vibrant woman.

The following poem is about a day they spent together just before her mother had been diagnosed:

The Peonies are in Full Bloom

Our day in the sun,
vivid, as if it were yesterday;
soft pink pedals
and the warmth of spring, caressing me.
It makes me wonder if you already knew,
at that day in the sun,
our brunch at Moutarde —
eating chocolate crepes and fresh fruit,
and laughing together,
like little girls —
it was almost too good to be true. I think maybe you knew.

Dawn Gunther

What is my intention for writing today?

____

____

____

What would I like to create or attract in my life?

____

____

____

What issues would I like to explore, honor or commit to?

____

____

____

You may want to repeat this until you have clarified your answer to a point where it is a statement that can become one of your affirmations.

You improve the quality of life in part by committing to the daily *work* . . . perhaps waking earlier than usual to meditate or write in a journal. Generate energy by abstaining from negative thoughts, emotions, and behaviors. This involves maintaining vigilance. Continued renewal of your commitment to change awakens the true self.

EXERCISE:

Sit comfortably in your chosen space. Light a candle if you desire. Take a deep breath. Exhale. Come into a meditative, grounded state. Inhale and know that the practice of writing unhinges stuck places. Take a few, deep cleansing breaths.

Breathe in. Dismiss judgments about how trivial, worrisome, or dire your issue might seem. Release. Breathe in the **willingness** to look at all this in a new way, to view this situation with a wide-angled lens. This is all that is needed. You may not know how to change, how to improve your situation or past; be open to the possibility of changing your perspective. Exhale.

First allow yourself to access a negative pattern, habit or wound which comes before your mind's eye. Drift over the situation, letting the vision come clearly into focus as details emerge.

Now watch a slow-motion video replaying this image. Who were you when this behavior was formed? Did you take comfort from others, try to get fulfillment from excess food or other substances? Did you seek solace from someone who couldn't give it?

Write in the voice of who you were at the time you first became aware of this thought or behavior. Can you recall when the habit first formed? Was it in response to some real or imagined threat? Was it for protection? Let the pen flow, remembering that memory and the imagination come from the same part of the brain. Invent what you cannot remember.

After twenty minutes, bring what you've written to closure. Jot down a few extra notes if there is more to say so you can resume writing on this topic some other time. Ask what this session has revealed.

I've discovered

____

____

____

____

Affirmation:

I am an intelligent, mature person who, as an adult, accepts where I am in life. I choose a healthy state of being.

Writing in this way provides the opportunity to reframe past patterns, wounds and experiences. This enables you to experience the present, clear of preconditioned attitudes. It adjusts hearts, souls and minds bringing them into alignment and it allows for the formulation of new intentions.

Awareness illuminates thought, emotion and impulse. "Why is this happening to me?" is dropped as you develop more penetrating questions, such as, "What does this pattern have to tell me?" and "How can I approach this situation differently?"

What writing can do, which makes a critical difference in health and well-being, is to give greater control of the mind and a broader understanding of the tricks it can play. Being aware of the chatter and not listening to the fruitless voices, perhaps more than anything, is what leads to this area of transformation. The nonsensical mind loves to be in control with its babble and tricks. It is sometimes referred to (especially in the middle of the night) as monkey-mind. If the brain is allowed to run rampant it spouts a lot of flawed information and lower-level thinking habits, keeping it in judgment and negativity.

Helpful to understanding why our minds perpetuate poor habits is the topic of neuron pathways. Neurons are roadways in the brain. Scientists *used to* believe that the number of neurons was fixed early in life and only declined from there. It was believed that connections between different brain cells were formed during certain critical periods early in life and after that, the architecture couldn't be modified. If you learned a way of being, it stuck.

With advanced understanding and research, scientists now talk about "neuron-plasticity". Research has shown that the brain is capable of building paths at any age. Neurons form new connections among themselves and the more one does something, the stronger these neural links become. Scientists have also learned that the body can create neurons from undifferentiated cells that are found even in elderly adults. If your awareness leads to the desire for change, with practiced effort, you can achieve what you wish.

By creating improved messages and systematically strengthening them through repetition, you can form habits which will become so strong they can compete with older, more dysfunctional ones. Many researchers advise that we just leave them alone and focus on strengthening the new healthier ways which will take over and dominate the weaker patterns.

THE BEST VISUAL EXPERIMENT EVER

Imagine that we start off in life as a clear glass of water.

Over time, people drop negative thoughts and traumatic events into us which, like droppers of ink, pollute. Parents, teachers, other kids, clergy, relatives, even strangers can rupture our well-being and self-esteem.

How to get rid of these toxic thoughts, feelings, memories and beliefs?

The murky ink is mixed with the water and therefore no longer separate. The only thing to do is to keep pouring in more clear water.

Then, watch the ink rise to the surface and wash away. It is possible to restore the happy clarity and trust we experienced as children.

Writing is a catalyst for speeding this process. As we write what is positive in our lives and what we are grateful for we change our nature. This doesn't mean that we are suddenly healed, receive a check in the mail or attract our soul mate. It means that we appreciate what we have which, in turn attracts more clarity. Clarity is a healthy, positive outlook….

Some ways in which I may effortlessly pour cool, clear water over something specific being dealt with now are:

____

____

____

____

____

____

____

____.

Please check out the fabulous work done by Harvard professor Shawn Achor on his web site **www.shawnachor.com**. I suspect that you will be delighted and surprised at the entertaining way he describes psychological research on positive change and its relationship to potential and happiness.

One of my strongest and most determined students, Rachel, had been raped while in college. Therapy helped a bit, but she felt that she was still consumed by hate and fear. For the first few weeks she came to class that was all she wrote about but she was determined to keep trying. She learned to trust that there would be a bottom to her rage.

One day, she was writing about the horror of being taken, half-dead, to the emergency room. She found herself writing about one particular nurse's kindness and how it had touched her. She suddenly realized that she was grateful to be alive. She started the process of getting in touch with gratitude more and found that she still had the potential to be happy once more. "It became so that I flooded myself with all that was good in my life and the sick individual who harmed me washed away. I can't say that I'm up to the part where I forgive him…I just don't give any thought or energy to him anymore."

Give up the illusion of being in control of what happens or changing what has occurred or what is factual! Focus on your process and learn the art of practicing faith. Just as worrying is wasted energy, so is trying to control outcomes. Instead, substitute a change of attitude. That can be controlled. The first approach is results-oriented, seeking a desired outcome, but one that we ultimately can't control which is a formula for frustration. The second approach, like setting an intention, is akin to creating a master plan. Remember that we are overriding extremely strong forces. Change takes determination, practice and patience.

Focus and let the outcome take care of itself. Be willing to feel empowered and loving towards yourself and others, no matter what the result may be. You may *want* to feel forgiveness but don't. The idea could feel repugnant for quite some time before you experience a shift. It is normal to experience reluctance towards letting go of blame. There can be the fear that our wounds won't be recognized. Honor the battle and remember to consciously release guilt, self-blame and doubt.

Clarissa had broken up with her fiancé a year before she came to class. She had called it quits and brought closure to the relationship, for the second time. She is someone who has been working through her issues by writing for a long time. After three or four months of grieving she started dating again, but the time just wasn't right. Instead of focusing on her dating failures, she concentrated on her girlfriends, tennis and her growing consulting business. But she was still miserable. "I find myself thinking of Larry all the time," she told me.

"You know how to stop it…don't give it energy and replace the thoughts with new positive ones. Write about what's right in your life…what you want to have happen."

"It's hard," she wailed.

"It's challenging," I corrected. "Every time he comes to your consciousness gently blow him away, realizing that your mind is playing tricks to make you recall things that upset you. This is an old habit and self-indulgent behavior."

I could say that to her because Clarissa is someone who had been writing and exploring her process by herself for years, so when she called the next month and said, "Done. I've handled it!" I was pleased but not surprised. She had allowed herself an evening of feeling everything from her past that this relationship triggered. She wrote it all out, allowing herself to cry as much as she needed to and then would think only positive thoughts the rest of the day. Every time she caught herself daydreaming or taunting herself she would replace that thought. She repeated the same procedure daily for the entire month.

Be patient with yourself as it takes time. This is the Mt. Everest of self change! We need to be strong and focused, but it is definitely worth the ascent.

This process may be likened to pushing yourself to exercise, or doing chores. The benefits are obvious but so is the resistance. I have to allow two to three hours of procrastinating, calling friends, cleaning a closet or polishing copper before I finally sit down to write. Allow plenty of wiggle room and make it easy until the benefits of writing deepen. You may then notice feeling so much better and find yourself simply making the time you need to reflect on the page. This is a sure sign that some kind of transformation is taking place. I have to plan to be home for the entire day, indulge myself with reading in the morning, walking in the afternoon and having something delicious in the evening in order to write a substantial amount! Then there are times I only manage to write at red lights.

Intensity or anger over a situation can actually ignite the psychological process and help sustain the discipline. Pound a few pillows or wait for the anger to flare before grabbing your notebook and pen.

I am always impressed by how many students dealing with the medical profession rid themselves of pent-up anger towards their doctors or lawyers once they begin writing. They often compose letters or scripts of things they wanted to say to the professionals but didn't because of fear that their treatment would be affected. Whether or not they ever send the letter is inconsequential. The key is to write it all out, to stop internalizing.

Where are grief and anger stored? The thymus is the gland near the base of your throat where it is said that grief resides. Try to release this emotion with conscious breathing after each writing exercise where anger flares.

EXERCISE:

Breathe in.

Envision the color pink.

Breathe out imagining the breath leaving through the thymus.

Breathe into this area again as you imagine that your breath is a balm to all pain.

Focus on the thymus gland, releasing all that is blocking your serenity. Allow your heart to open and for some area of grief to loosen. Breathe in the color pink.

As you breathe out imagine one segment of self-contained sorrow floating up and out. Breathe new energy into this area. Breathe out remaining anguish you feel safe enough to release.

Now think of an incident from your childhood which has caused you sorrow. It could be as simple as a childhood slight on the playground. If this event came to your conscious now then take the time to honor and examine it.

After writing and reading what you recorded see if you can look at the situation with new compassion and understanding for your young self. Be careful not to experience prolonged regret (another time-wasting activity) and remember that your experiences have brought you to the present moment. Release with some purposeful breathing. You may want to return to do this exercise often during times of extreme stress or misery.

Even after doing all the work, when faced with a dilemma or crisis you may still sometimes feel as if you have lost your coping skills.

Stephanie had been bereft for longer than she realized. "All of my wisdom is in a box high on a shelf-I can't access it. I've lost all my "tools," she moaned. "No you haven't-you've just lost the key," I told her. She then wrote the story of how she was always kept as a 'doll.' She had gone from her girlhood home to the life she created with her loving, caring husband. When he became ill she felt as if she was adrift.

"Write down the story," I said, "so you can see it objectively." After months of writing Stephanie was able to reframe her journey. She realized that she was capable of finding what she needed to unlock any door. She was finished seeing herself as a toy on a shelf and was anxious to start living as an adult woman. By telling her story and receiving the group's support she was able to relocate her ability to cope.

To see the hurt we've suffered and acknowledge it is a key to the healing process. We just want to know that our journeys matter.

What are some other keys?

____

____

____

____

____

____.

Writing about memories that are less than pleasant may reactivate thoughts and feelings of having been wronged or betrayed. Revisiting an incident could also bring realizations of personal responsibility, guilt or misunderstanding. Sometimes we tell ourselves that we might have made things turn out differently, but maybe we really couldn't have stopped what transpired. We just make ourselves believe this and actually keep a negative, addictive, punitive loop spinning.

Often when childhood wounds are revisited with an adult's awareness it becomes evident that as children we were truly powerless. This is where compassion for that small, impressionable child is developed. We have been carrying around the pain, and the story, all this time. This may severely affect how current dilemmas or circumstances are handled. If willing to release the story we literally become lighter and more able to cope with the present. (Ever hear the one about angels being able to fly because they take themselves lightly?)

Another tale is of two Buddhist monks who walked along a shallow stream. They came upon a wailing woman lying by the edge of the shore. "Why are you crying, my child?" asked one. "I must get to the other side, to find my mother, but am afraid of the water." "I will carry you," said the same monk and he did. He left her safely on the other shore. Then, after walking for miles, the other monk asked, "Why did you carry the woman, it is a sin to have bodily contact with women." The monk replied, "I left the woman at the shore an hour ago but you still carry her."

Realize that it is time to put your burdens down, that it is safe to stop carrying them. You did the best you could with the information you had at the time. Now let all that go. Lovingly detach.

Elissa had been coming to class at the suggestion of her therapist. "A few years ago I was asked by my attorney to write a dossier of events leading up to the wrongdoing involved in a family inheritance. I was to recall events that had happened long before. The four pages that flowed from me in long-hand were a painful reminder of family history. I wisely let it go for the rest of the day but awoke the next morning, knowing that I had to type it up and fax it to the attorney. I was tired thinking of how I had been there for everyone all those years and feeling indignant that I wasn't appropriately provided for."

She told us that she had paced the entire morning, going aimlessly from room to room. "I had another cup of decaf coffee. My nerves were quite shot from the two years that this ordeal had been taking place. I was filled with guilt, frustration and shame. I had been brought up to keep family business within the family."

She called her cousin, an attorney, to ask her advice and to read her what she had written. "She gave me a few pointers and then stated quietly and simply, 'The judge will clearly see what you are describing.' Then she named what had been taking place as abuse."

"I went to the computer consoled but still nervous. When I finished, I was sobbing. I had revealed a long family history of hidden dysfunction. We had never called it that. After all, it wasn't sexual or what we label as physical abuse but on the page, factually recorded without embellishment or analysis, was a portrayal of intimidation, manipulation, falsehoods and deception. It was the first time I was able to see and name it for what it was. Writing it down and looking at it was startling but also liberating."

"The truth shall set you free," says the Bible. "We are as sick as our sickest secrets," says John Bradshaw.

Elissa is someone for whom the writing process has been torture. Yet, she keeps coming back. She wrote, "It took a number of miserable days until I was willing to let all the information sink in without *it* sinking *me*. What I finally felt from the unburdening was enormous relief. I was beginning to feel self-compassion."

Writing can rid us of the topics that have been suppressed but have had a powerful effect. Cleansing and renewal can be achieved through issue-charged writing.

Come into the present empty, quiet and clear. This is calm. This is peace.

It may take time for the full impact of what you've suffered to completely surface. Give yourself space and awareness. Be vigilant during this period of time; watch for signs of extra stress or unexpected sadness. It is normal. Take extreme self-care (read Chapter Five).

The good news is that with a writing practice you can experience the entire process of healing. Remember to acknowledge how the past feeds the present. Just as in nature there is a period of time before a stem takes root, so it is with healing. Allow as much time as you need without getting stuck, or root-bound. When ready, rake back the mulch and allow the blossoming to begin.

Twenty minutes of writing without attaching to the feelings which surface may become as integral a part of everyday maintenance as tooth brushing.

Try these two exercises while being alert to how you feel before and after the writing.

Exercise:

You may want to do this exercise in bed, or snuggled on the sofa. Settle in and gently shut your eyes. Think of a children's song that you used to love. Which one comes to mind immediately? ***London Bridges? Frere Jacques? You Are My Sunshine?***

Imagine yourself singing. How old are you in this scene? Where is this taking place and what are you wearing? Who else is there?

Visualize the beautiful child you are. Do you need anything? What is healthy, nurturing and comforting? Think about each area of your life such as nutrition, sleep, exercise, taking a bath, being with friends, resting when you are tired or having to take an emotional health day. How many of the habits you practice now were started back then? Do you give to yourself now in a healthy way? Play around with the idea that you are going to pamper this child in the most supportive, most deserving way you can imagine. When you feel ready come back in to the room and record all that you saw yourself doing and how others treated you at that time. Then write about how you care for yourself now and what changes, if any, you are prepared to make in order to live in a more supportive, nurturing way.

Be Sure To:

1. Allow time and space for each writing session. Trying to cram too much into the time allotted will alter the essence of what could be achieved.
2. Remember to create a pre-writing ritual and tailor it to suit your needs. It could be a warm shower or bath, a cup of tea or coffee, a short nap or meditation.
3. Set aside reward time after a session, in case you need emotional R&R. You may want to just rest quietly, take a walk or do anything that is meditative after unearthing memories and perhaps digesting new perspectives and understanding.

Often we ignore or lose our way while attending to others. We nurture spouses, children siblings and parents, often ignoring ourselves. Cynthia is a hospice nurse who helps others all the time, guiding them to a sense of wholeness and peace. She called recently to tell me that she would not be in class the next day because she was exhausted.

"It doesn't have to be that way," I replied in what I hoped was a gentle tone.

She was a widow who was now just rejoining the dating scene. She went on, "I'm just so anxious. There's a knot in my stomach when I think about dating. I don't know how to care for myself in a way that makes me feel attractive."

"What feeling is under the knot?" I asked.

"I never have time to get ready. I need to take care of myself and don't have the time. And anyway, none of them measures up to Jack. This one doesn't talk well, that one slumps, another doesn't kiss well…the list goes on and on. I'm angry at Jack for dying."

"That's what you need to write about," I suggested.

"I don't know who I'm supposed to be aside from being married or a widow. I'm afraid. I think that I just have to go through this."

"You don't have to suffer through it. Write your way through it," I suggested. She was silent. "Write to Jack and tell him how you feel. Ask for his advice. From what you've told me, I think he would want you to find happiness again, he'd understand your anger and encourage you to really care for yourself."

"I think I will make it to class tomorrow," she said softly.

EXERCISE:

Allow yourself to settle in. Come to your awareness of the breath. Inhale. Take a moment to thank your breath for nurturing and caring for you without your even being aware of it most of the time.

Exhale. Think of how you have taken care of others, sometimes at the expense of your own well being.

Inhale. Ask yourself if you live for others at the sacrifice of yourself. Exhale.

Identify some ways in which you may do this.

____

____

____

____

____.

After writing sit back and ask yourself if you are at peace. If not, ask what you have to do in order to get to that graced state of being. Be honest with yourself and ask if you are willing to do what is takes to be purposeful and peaceful.

Breathe in now and ask on the deepest level as well as the most obvious one, why you believe you are here and what you believe your purpose is now. To appreciate life and be grateful; to express your given talents is one answer. To teach, to heal, to enlighten, to nurture…the list goes on and on. Slowly and gently open your eyes; express in writing what you feel you are here for, in this lifetime.

If you've never thought of your life as having a purpose, now is the time to do so. Victor Frankl, the renowned psychologist, discovered this profound lesson as an inmate in the concentration camps during the Holocaust. He realized that all could be taken from him except his purpose. He saw many victims survive torture and humiliation only to live long enough to bring the monsters who tortured them to justice. He witnessed others whose will lasted in order to find surviving members of their families. Some lived to tell their stories. Frankl's research in the camps found that people who perished were the ones who were weakened from lack of purpose. Those who survived found that it didn't matter whether it was a positive or negative motivation that kept them going-just as long as there was a commitment to it.

Breathe in now and ask on the deepest level as well as the most obvious one, why you believe you are here and what you believe your purpose is now. To appreciate life and be grateful for it as expressed by your given talents is one answer. To teach, to heal, to enlighten, to nurture...the list goes on and on. Writing about our losses and pain in story form can also greatly enhance our lives. As these linked experiences of pain and recovery are added to one another, layer upon layer, we realize the intricacy of our lives and we are enriched. Benefits may increase as we relay what we have endured. In the retelling we step back and observe through objective eyes and heart.

"Thought transcends matter" the playwright, Henrik Ibsen said. Holding on to the past instead of setting down any fear, anger, or hurt, can impede living in the moment. Learning how to accept the present situation is liberating. It is then possible to move forward with purpose. The universe is supportive of this courage. Walk with respect and love for what you have lived through and how you have triumphed. Walk through to the other side of pain, then look back to see that what was once heavy and painful is now transformed into something much lighter.

AFFIRMATION:

I am an intelligent, peaceful, creative adult who can change or accept anything.

SUMMARY:

- Storytelling with intention can create new meaning and purpose in life.
- Focus on the process and the practice of faith.
- Remember to be patient with each step of the journey.
- Practice viewing stored up emotion from a detached vantage point.

CHAPTER THREE:

WAKE UP AND MAKE UP

Reconciliation with Your Past

It's never too late to have a happy childhood.
— Gloria Steinem

Many of us grew up in emotionally toxic environments. Doubt, trauma and insecurity might have been reasons enough not to deal with life's challenges wisely. Sometimes negative thinking led to incorrect or unhealthy perceptions. But negativity need not control any longer…if you wake up and choose differently, right now; it is not too late!

If we are not handling present reality in a healthy, loving way there is usually an underlying emotion fueling the dysfunction. Procrastination, laziness and lack of self worth (these are not from lack of character) can act as a control, blocking the courage needed to conquer demons. Then there's denial, the imaginary escape chute.

The problems will continue to crop up throughout life until a critical situation, or awareness, demands that notice finally be taken. Each time an issue returns it is stronger, louder and more challenging to address. Anna Freud, Sigmund's psychologist daughter, wrote that in the beginning of a young person's journey the universe gives wide berth to explore and make mistakes; corridors narrow and the consequences become more severe as we continue down the path.

When exploring the past in writing, be aware that you might not have been equipped with the skills needed for wise choices. You might have been powerless, frightened or helplessly ignorant when paths were forged. So much energy might have been needed to deal with survival or self-protection. Compassion is the peace which heals the war within.

EXERCISE:

Inhale as you direct your body to relax. Exhale.
As you inhale once again watch your thoughts drift by without attaching to any of them. Exhale.

Inhale deeply, feeling a connection with the ground beneath you. Exhale and identify a negative thought, feeling or belief about yourself that is willing to release. Realize that it no longer serves you. You will only let go of what feels safe to relinquish.

Inhale deeply and as you exhale, watch the ribbons of negative energy unravel. Inhale fresh, clear air. Are you are aware of having carried these behaviors and beliefs for a very long time, perhaps since childhood? Exhale.

Breathe deeply, imagining that the tips your fingers are tiny spigots. Visualize turning each one on as toxins from your past flow out and wash away. Breathe.

If the feeling of emptying out is uncomfortable, remember that you are now filled with the clean, clear water of all the new programming and positive self-talk.

Locate a situation from your past where events were less than satisfactory. Did you see yourself as a victim, or as judgmental and envious? Were you taught to compare yourself to others? Using your new awareness ask if you felt invisible or unworthy at the time. Are you perhaps still harboring negative feelings in your memory? Do you see the incident as you did when it occurred, without the benefit of your current wisdom?

When you have finished with your completed remembrance, come back to the room. Begin to record the experience you just brought to the surface. When twenty minutes have passed or you feel that you are done (some choose to keep writing if they have not finished in the suggested time), take a moment and read what is on the page. Make note of what emotions have emerged: anger, sadness, grief, shame or guilt? What has been in the way of reconciling with the past? Remember that you do not actually have to contact others. Your resolution just needs you to be present.

Close your eyes again and visualize the sun's rays as if they are streaming directly into your heart, filling you with light and energy… now rest.

What would it take for you to forgive yourself and everyone else who has caused you pain?

Gloria shared that she wasn't able to write about her husband who had died quite suddenly, twelve years before she started coming to class.

When you mentioned the release of pain I didn't think that I needed to go there. I felt as if I had gotten past it, that I had the memory of his death cordoned off somewhere. Now that I have written some things I see that I was wrong. It is still raw. It is really running me and I haven't wanted to admit it. Everyone thinks that I am such a happy-go-lucky person. I don't want to disappoint them. How foolish. I'm suffering and those close to me know it anyway.

Forgiveness of ourselves and others may not completely surface on the page the first time we write but we need to be patient; the writing will eventually bring serenity. If we don't examine the reasons we are holding on to chronic pain and sadness we are withholding our own healing. There is no reward for staying stuck in pain except the familiarity of distress and deprivation.

When Gloria wrote again, the following week, she unearthed the belief that had been in her way: *I feel that I am not entitled to enjoy myself since my husband no longer can.*

Let us vanquish our refusal to let our lives flow. Create an affirmation such as:

I am allowing right action to flow through me at all times
(no matter what is happening around me).

By releasing the guilt she felt for being alive, Gloria lifted the burden she had been dragging with her for years.

Loretta said, *I'm learning that life doesn't need to be lived on a tightrope. It can be enjoyed on a wide plank. I always felt that I was trying to knit with Jello before. Now I see that I just wasn't having my needs met by others, and most of all, by myself.*

No one else can travel *your* journey; keep coming back to *your* self. Keep asking what your needs are. When in sadness, do you need those who love you to listen without offering help or advice, or do you need them to provide actual guidance? Learn what works best and ask for it. This is your time to recuperate.

I remember going through a particularly trying time and calling my dear friend Sue when I needed a verbal hug. I realized that I reached out for her more than the others and wondered why. The next time I called I found out.

"Sue, I'm feeling hopeless. I know it will pass but it doesn't feel like it will," I cried.

"Aah, aah baby," she cooed. "Of course you feel lousy—what you're going through is horrid."

Since then I've been able to call Sue and say, "Three aah babies please!" We've spread the word amongst our nearest and dearest. Feel free to use this and establish your own comfort network. Write about what is most soothing to you and who best provides it, besides yourself. Ask for what you need!

EXERCISE:

Breathe slowly and steadily as you visualize friends and family floating past your consciousness. Notice if you need to adjust your posture in order to feel rooted and focused.

Inhale. Who in your life nurtures you? Who is supportive? Exhale. Take another breath. In your mind's eye, are you seeing anyone who feels toxic to you? What about your mother-in-law? Or, your mother? A sister, friend, doctor, daughter or aunt? Is there anyone in your life at present less than supportive, uplifting or kind? If so, exhale some of their negativity now. Spend less mental and emotional time with them.

If you are able to release what is dismissive or hurtful about them, do so now.

Slowly, allow yourself to re-enter the room and begin to write a letter to one of these people, revealing what is troubling you. **Keep coming back to your needs.** Claim closure. Remember that you are not necessarily going to send this letter.

Some people keep these letters tucked away and then review them after time. They have reported the growing detachment they feel, often marveling that the pain has all but disappeared. In some cases, people have chosen to distance themselves from their unhealthy relationships. In a few instances, reconciliation has occurred without the other person even being aware of the process. What matters is the choice to feel peace and non-attachment, no matter what.

Am I committed to being joyful, creative and inspired?

____.

What am I willing to give up and what do I imagine will replace the discomfort?

____

____

____.

I choose to be joyful

This is an affirmation to be repeated when dealing with difficult situations. Remember that a healthy relationship with yourself must come before all else, even though this might sound shallow at times. The *willingness* to exercise this choice is like one of those moving walkways at airports. It transports you, even as you're standing still.

What is an action you are willing to take or what are you willing to release, in order to experience joy?

____

____

____.

What are some "buts" which may pop up?

I choose to be joyful but __________________________

____.

I can't feel joyful because __________________________

____

____

____.

Insight must be translated into the language of the heart to be able to convert to change. Emotional issues take up residence in the body, as well as being housed in the mind. Writing takes this awareness to ever deeper levels. Through writing you integrate what intuitively is known to be true.

Even insight isn't always enough to break free of old patterns. There's usually a moment when you are ready to change yet find yourself held captive by an unseen force. Why is this unknown energy paralyzing just when you're ready to surge forward?

There are many reasons. Simply put, this force, the ego—is emotionally two years old. It is a feisty child who wants to be in control. It has too much at stake to let go. Befriend the ego as you did the critic and let it know of your strength. Thank it for protecting you over the years and reward it with a rest.

EXERCISE:

Breathe. Root your feet into the earth. Imagine the spine as a golden chord reaching up through the top of your head and into the sky. Feel both grounded and elevated so that you may activate both energies. Breathe. Open the area where dreams are formed. Be aware of energy awakening as you breathe.

Now think of an incident or relationship that is currently causing stress, pain or stuck energy. If there is nothing at the moment, go back in your memory to a situation with someone that habitually irks you (think of holidays as they often bring out the worst).

Is there a desire for change and healing? Recall the actions of other people involved; watch what you do. Observe without judgment or attachment. Ask for what you need.

Ask: What have I been attached to? Am I still looking for something from others that I need to learn to give to myself? Why keep going to these people for what they can't, or won't give?

Who am I committed to being no matter what? What do others have invested in me staying the same? Is there a trigger someone in my life pulls that keeps me stuck?

Come back to the room and begin to write; explore how things can turn out differently. What needs to change in order to bring about the desired result? Remember that you can't change others! Write about reclaiming your power.

After twenty minutes take a break. Leave the work for a while. Be the artist who turns the canvas to the wall.

When ready (and it may be a day or two) re-read with fresh eyes, a renewed mind. See something you hadn't noticed before? Do you now have insight into the situation where there had been none previously?

It is never the circumstance which causes distress but how we respond to it. Esteemed psychologist Dr. Bob Goldblatt has a wonderful exercise to utilize for any situation needing resolution. When feeling resistance, remorse, confusion, or any other painful emotion ask:

Am I strong...or weak?
Am I an adult...or a child?
Am I a woman...or a girl?
Am I smart...or ignorant?

Answering honestly may reveal childish, weak, stupid behavior, but the mere process of stopping to consider and recognizing the choices allows us to make the switch.

When finished ascertaining where you are in a given situation, affirm:

I am an intelligent, mature, talented woman who can get this job done.

Saying this once or twice hardly provides the motivation needed. Writing the message on a card and repeating it often halts the previous beliefs and actions. This does bring about change. I have found myself asking if an intelligent woman would be watching TV or eating Reese's Pieces instead of writing an important letter to resolve a situation.

During times of stress many of us abandon self-care. You may not get enough rest, you may get too much. Learn to trust that the writing will renew your energy and that motivation to rejoin life will manifest, even when dealing with grave illness or loss. It took Dawn many months after her mother's death to take up running again. She forced herself in the beginning until it became a habit once more. She was delightfully surprised when she sat down and wrote this touching tribute to her mom:

Running with Me

Today she was running with me
as my feet tapped the earth
arms drawing
air inward,
breath calming but tired and worn.

The voice that beckons from above
whispers in my heart with love;
and I, aching with soulful happiness,
feel my toes leap with ecstasy!

Like a dove I can fly high and finally see!

Oh, joy - her hair is auburn and glows!
Her flesh young, like snow
light and fresh;
radiant
and happy,

As I knew she always was

Laughing with glee
at the delight that is me
(or so a mom would say)
but she kept the joy for herself,
this time sparing me nothing
(if not for the syncopated rhythmic flight),
that used to be her melancholy.

Now shining like a light,
her smiling eyes emit true delight,
if only just to be with me
for just another night.

For just one more day,
or night,
shiny,

sparkling,
alive
and bright.

Dawn Gunther

Meditating with the written word will create more space to upgrade the quality of your inner conversation. Follow the call to write; express the pain before stagnation and dullness can take hold. Anyone who has gone through this can attest to the torturous nagging involved. Conversely, when the story is told the healing process is activated.

While journaling, ask: How was anger handled in my home when I was a child? Was I encouraged to express my upset? Was I shown how to channel aggression and rage? Were these emotions even acknowledged when I was young? Was there gender bias? ("Nice girls don't get angry.") Was I shown healthy ways to deal with these strong emotions? Where in my body has the pain lodged itself?

Louise Hay wrote her groundbreaking work in a highly recommended book, **You Can Heal Your Life** (New World Library; 2nd edition, 1995). In it she describes a very heart-wrenching tale of her childhood with a disturbed mother. Her story describes how she felt like a victim until taking control of her life. The end of the book contains a chart which ascribes metaphysical meaning to pain or illness. For instance, disease, pain or injury in the knees symbolizes fear of moving forward. Experiencing too much stress has been linked, no surprise here, with heart ailments. Affirmations are offered for each ailment to help remedy the mental or physical causation. The book is an eye-opening reference for anyone open to exploring a unique perspective.

In class, Delia has used journaling to access the primary cause of her obesity. *In my house frustration was dealt with by tranquilizing ourselves with food. As I keep writing about various daily habits and customs from my childhood I am able to locate my anger about not having a say, about being controlled. It was a very rigid household. My father was a high ranking official in the army. We had to eat at set hours, consume what was put in front of us and exercise when my father commanded. I hated my life and raged inside for years. No one knew that the sweet, cherubic child was really a wild demon beneath the surface. To keep us 'happy' my mother pried my sister and me with sweets. Mother ate everything and we did, also. It took me three years of treatment and therapy to lose 120 pounds. That was six years ago. I never get on a scale, binge or regurgitate anymore, but I am faithful to my daily journaling. It is here that I pour out my heart's frustration. I have come to accept what has passed and move on.*

What do *you* do with anger? How do you process it?

What is the trigger that most frequently causes you to get angry? Is it the lack of something (acknowledgment, justice)? While viewing the kernel of anger through this particular lens, explore when in your life the fury saved you.

____

____

____

____.

What do I need now to release any left-over, stuck emotion?

____

____

____.

What has it been brought to teach me?

____

____

____.

In class Loretta wrote, *Pain has taught me to move forward, to unknot what has me stuck. Let me rid this house of the divorce and all the stray pieces of pain. Let me find the end of the ball of yarn, take that one piece and start knitting the rest of my life with it.*

Megan, a visual artist used her pain to express the depths of despair and in the process found the emotion's beauty:

FLY AWAY

Open windows ready to fly
Here destiny is about to die
Spread My Wings I Have Done Too Long

Nothing seems to flow along
Smooth and clear I want to see
But You Have Taken All From Me
A Son A Child A Life and Hope
Burnt to a Crisp a Savage Pulp
Hell Insight this Boarded Flight
Away I Go Into the Night
Away Again to the Make-Believe
So Many Times I've been Deceived
You Make a Claim and Check it Twice
Make Sure It Hurts Twice as Nice
Who Ever Thought I Could Survive

Megan Siranni Brand

EXERCISE:

Think of a time in your life when a particular behavior saved you from abuse, ridicule, or neglect. Perhaps you were the child who went with the flow to keep peace. Are you Still doing this? Are you suffering from not getting in touch with a strong emotion?

____

____.

WHAT YOU CAN DO NOW

Scan your body. Is there any place you are holding pain or burdens? How much is on your plate?

Ask: Am I weighed down by responsibilities?

Lighten your thoughts by raising your vibrations. Happy thoughts equal a higher frequency; this is a real challenge in difficult times. Will-power!

Prioritize. Choose three things you absolutely must do today; reschedule the rest.

Do Affirmations. Break for exercise. Think inspiring thoughts.

Give and be open to receiving. You must do both to be complete. Is being receptive a difficult task? Is being generous a challenge?

Can you lift your energy?

Create the space to honor and give to your self. Know that as you do you are more apt to help those you touch with an act of kindness, a smile, a laugh. The ripple of this travels far. Radiate your love both inwards and out into the world, no matter what is going on in your life; it is amazing the effect this can have.

In writing strive to express your own thoughts and feelings with depth. Speak for the unhealed child who couldn't find the words when they were needed. A soulful method of writing devised by Linda Metcalf and Toby Simon, former English professors at Pratt Institute in New York is called Proprioceptive Writing. They teach their innovative and profound method to interested artists, educators and laymen. Their worthwhile work is described at www.pwriting.org.

Old memories, beliefs and feelings may seem to be fossilized. Yet, for the elders at an independent living home who choose to come to my memoir writing workshop, there is a surprising lack of rigidity. This allows for an easy flow of ideas and feelings in most of the participants. The residents come from various backgrounds and belief systems. They might not have been able to sit down and be candid with each other at any other time in their lives. Open, positive and grateful are these particular grandmothers who have lived through the Depression, Holocaust, deaths, widowhood and perhaps, some memory loss.

Most walk through the doors of the residence's library excited about expressing themselves. Some come to unburden, others to record memories for themselves and their families. There is majesty to these women who express their own version of what has transpired in their lifetimes. They, for the most part, are modest and authentic, not realizing the magnitude of their own wisdom.

Once we wrote about faith and solace after discussing the transcendental poets. Mrs. Smith, the most gracious and regal of attendees, shared that she is currently familiarizing herself with the poet Emerson and is struck by his steadfast beliefs. Emerson proclaimed the healing power of journaling and how his intuition always presented solutions to life's dilemmas. She recalled that faith had never been discussed in her Episcopalian home, that her parents had never attended church. She wrote that she is working on developing faith now. "When I asked my mother about church and religion, I recall her telling me that I could see how I felt when called upon to explore that part of life. Fancy that...I'm interested now, all these years later. I find that I have to work at finding it."

Gertie who is Jewish, often regales us with stories as heartwarming as S'holem Aleichem's, "I've always had faith," she stated. "It's always been a part of me, I guess." Good humor and interest in others cloaks her concern over physical discomfort and pain.

Highly intelligent and still inquisitive, AJ is of Irish-Catholic descent. She is steeped in the ways of the church and the Christian faith. It has been her only option for dealing with life's struggles, she tells us. Mother, step-mother and grandmother; I am amazed watching her strength-in-action upon being widowed for a second time.

They sit and discuss what each has written about religious thought and experiences. They say that they feel happier in general now, than at any other time of life. They all want to learn from the others.

I marvel that these ladies do not complain, or regret what has been. Vital in their thoughts, emotions and experiences, they take their various philosophies and come to a greater understanding of themselves and each other. They are exquisite in their flexibility and radiance. They glow as they wake to engaging ideas and youthful memories.

Bonding through their writing, they recall past grief and celebrate triumph over adversity. Through sheer determination, day by day, year by year, they have lived well. We talk about how good memories bring joy to the surface once more, refreshing in the moment of rediscovery. Sometimes the memories, too painful to have been discussed before, are now displayed like old war injuries. The women are proud and no longer feel pain from the past.

As these writers live together there is magic when they open up and reveal parts of themselves. They open presents for each other with each revelation. "I didn't know that about you!" is heard often as each woman reads. I have seen the miracle of healing more than once and it still amazes me.

Once, Minnie wrote about losing a child to typhoid fever. She was wistful but not overwhelmed. As she read to the group Geraldine, a lovely woman who was always enveloped by melancholy, got up from her seat and went to sit next to her. "I lost a child also," she said in almost a whisper. She didn't say anything else but continued to sit next to Minnie instead of returning to her seat for the rest of the session. As the group dispersed the two women stayed, talking. They held hands as they reminisced.

When I told the story to the activity director, she was astounded. "Geraldine never spoke of her son's death. Her children told us that she never got over it. They said it explained her bouts of depression. She has been here three years this month. I can't believe she spoke of it."

Not only did she speak to Minnie but the two became fast friends. Geraldine wrote about her son and his death more and more, bit by bit, over time. We all watched as she lightened up and her sadness lessened tremendously. Geraldine was ninety at the time. She had been thirty when her child had perished in a fire. At centers, in my private workshops, at Gilda's, universities; anywhere there are people willing to open up, express their pain or show up against the odds, healing has taken place.

You can always unburden, refine, revise, and reshape your view of what has transpired in life.

EXERCISE:

Breathe a few deep breaths.

What images, beliefs, feelings or concerns from your past are here with you today? Breathe. Were you brought up with a faith in a greater power? Allow yourself to drift now to a time in childhood when things didn't work out in a desired way. Were you able to have faith that all would eventually work out? Were you able to be patient? Take time drifting until an experience or conversation surfaces. Then come slowly back to the room, keeping a soft focus on the page. Pick up the pen or pencil and describe what has surfaced in your mind's eye. Stay supple within, allowing thoughts and feelings to emerge on the page.

After reading what has been written, remember that if there was faith at some point in life it always returns. If there hasn't been faith and it is desired, develop the belief that the universe will provide if there is a willingness to trust this principle.

Through recalling memories you can deal with handicapped or underdeveloped parts of yourself which have long been buried. All you need is the intention to do so. What is your intention for today's session? What is it you would like to create or attract in life? Is there an issue to be explored, honored, committed to or reframed?

When strengths are recognized you are more apt to accept pain, fear, confusion and loss. When released, peace and inner joy are available. Some ascribe to the belief that you are only given that which you can handle; the rest of us scream for help when confronted by an excess of stress. Sometimes you must interact with people who drain life force, often unknowingly. The following exercise allows you to create a shield for protection in times of vulnerability.

Exercise:

With eyes closed and your mind on the breath, envision a field of wildflowers, next to the ruins of a medieval abbey. Stand viewing the ruins, observing the crumbling stone and the jagged rocks. Watch as clouds float by.

Look down and see a shield lying on the ground. What does it look like? Is it iron, brass, aluminum, steel or gold? Notice that it has two pieces - a front and a back. Are both sides the same? Are they bejeweled? Take the time and visualize just what you want or need. Allow the talisman to speak, for it will go where you need to go. You can carry this protection for the rest of life's journey. Imagine donning this object before you go out into the world each day. Imagine surrounding yourself with the front and back pieces when embarking upon any adventure from now on.

Slowly open your eyes and begin to describe the image. Write about the message of protection presented. Recall a time when you *did* feel protected. What qualities (they may be metaphoric, symbolic or literal) had to be present to feel this way? Include these in the description. See a message inscribed on the surface? For example: I am shielded by my faith. I am protected and guided. I say yes to whatever may happen; I am safe.

Eyes closed once more, drift back to a time when you felt threatened or unprotected. Now picture a large, shiny, translucent bubble, the kind blown from those wands most loved by children. The bubble grows somewhat larger than you were when this frightening event or feeling was present.

Step lightly into the bubble as it closes behind, securing you within. Float comfortably where no one can harm you. Stay here for as long as it feels appropriate. When ready come back gently into the room and begin to describe what fears prevailed when feeling unprotected and exposed.

Write about the experience from within the bubble. Visualize stepping into one at any time, for however long and whenever needed in the present. This is a particularly powerful tool to utilize when interacting with troublesome people or situations.

PAST BELIEFS

You do have free will of thought. Will negative or frustrating thoughts ever take place? Of course. Can you observe yourself and switch? Yes. Do you always believe you can? No, of course not, especially if you have had a life of thinking otherwise. But you can shift the balance a majority of the time.

Become aware of where your focus usually is and where it would best serve. This is a lifelong process, not unlike replacing fries with salad as the metabolism slows down and awareness picks up! It all has to do with perspective and what is embraced as a prosperous viewpoint.

Examine what your childhood beliefs were around prosperity. How many of these beliefs are outdated? Have they brought joy or woe, sadness, worry, security or generosity? When you realize that abundance is a state of mind, 'scarcity thinking' and worry can be minimized, perhaps even eliminated.

What is meant by prosperity? I take it to mean feeling unconditional love and acceptance, while acknowledging and appreciating what is real. Reflect upon the childhood messages that surrounded this very crucial aspect of existence; observe how they colored all of life and how they may need some alteration or replacement.

EXERCISE:

Close your eyes and let the breath take you back to a childhood scene or belief surrounding prosperity, or its lack. This is where you can locate the origins of your current beliefs. When you are ready, return to your pen and recreate the scenario with a child's vision. Then add adult insight.

Take yourself off the whipping post of life. Whenever we compare ourselves to others we are lost.

"You sound stressed," someone told Claire in class one day as she rattled on about everything from the traffic to the weather. "I am," she whined. "I am being tested, challenged and am struggling with a situation involving my entire history. Family. It involves betrayal, manipulation, victimization, lack of responsibility, lying, cheating and money," Claire announced. "Other than hanging, do you have any suggestions?" "Are you writing?" we all cried out in unison.

Over the next two months Claire demurred from bringing the issue to class. Then she announced, *I've been doing better than I, or anyone who knows me, ever imagined I would. My writing is cheering me on and I am learning to embrace the struggle as I sharpen every fiber of my being. I see what the stress was doing to me mentally, physically and emotionally, now I adjust when the awareness surfaces. I use meditation, chocolate and other things in my ever-building arsenal. The bouts of utter frustration are less and less frequent in me.*

Suzanne is someone else who is learning that writing can accompany her through life with a severely handicapped child and a mother with dementia. Suzanne was a high fashion model and is married to an extremely successful, loving businessman. She recently wrote about how she copes. *My life has not been easy. Much more difficult than people can imagine. You know what gets me through? Focus. Through writing I have learned how to focus on happy things or on something totally unrelated to my past and what I have endured. I allow the writing to take my concentration.*

Another student, Maggie wrote: *Through my commitment to finally practicing gratitude and all the other forms of wisdom, I have been led to where I desperately wanted to be. I was so focused on embracing the struggle that the struggle slipped away and I hadn't even noticed.*

I focused on the positive until the negative atrophied and withered away, Reba recalled. *Has this been permanent? Heck, no. Like a weed, it will crop up and grow. You know we must be the vigilant gardener and nurture only that which we want to grow.*

Take yourself seriously, but lighten up while doing it.

CONCENTRATION: *The Art of Compartmentalizing*

You can learn to focus on the here and now by learning how to compartmentalize. This is also an excellent way to stop worrying or obsessing about the past.

Write four things you are worrying about now. Write the first things that come to mind:

1. ______________________________
2. ______________________________
3. ______________________________
4. ______________________________

Write five things you think about that are in the past (could be resentments, grudges, lost dreams, missed opportunities, betrayals, abuses, etc.):

1. ______________________________
2. ______________________________
3. ______________________________
4. ______________________________
5. ______________________________

Write four or five things that are habitual worries:

1. ______________________________
2. ______________________________
3. ______________________________
4. ______________________________
5. ______________________________

Finally, close your eyes. Imagine a dresser of drawers or a file cabinet. Visualize it vividly. See yourself putting each of the things bothering you now in the drawers. Think about whether you can attend to any of these things today. Is there anything you can do to help you appreciate and enjoy the day? Come back to the room and describe everything revealed through the writing. What have you discovered?

Students tell me that they physically feel different after doing this work. Writing about issues allows you to be the witness instead of the victim. *Seeing how I perceived things before I started writing and now that I've done it for this semester changes me,"* Vanessa said. *"People tell me I look different. Brighter and lighter are two of the words I hear most often.*

When the words are seen on paper, not only the tale but also the depth and breadth of the story, new insights which lead to wisdom are revealed. Then if the hard-earned lessons are shared others will benefit also. Both culturally, and in my nuclear family, we were taught to look for humor–black, dry, slapstick or witty. This has been a balm for many wounds. Mostly it has allowed me to shift a story's perspective and release the pain. My childhood was painful in the living but funny in the retelling.

My Mother's Daughter

As I was maturing, one of my biggest fears was that I would turn into my mother, who I experienced during my teen years as an angry, critical person, someone who was never satisfied with me. "Why can't you bake gingerbread cookies like Lil's daughter?" my mother once asked me. At 13, I just shrugged. I was made to feel inadequate because I didn't like to bake.

Now it's 2010, I am 67 and my mother is 94. When she developed mild dementia at age 90 and could no longer live alone in Florida, we got help. Then the money ran out. Now she lives with me, her oldest daughter. My husband, who watched his father deteriorate in a nursing home from Parkinson's disease, agrees having her here is the right thing to do—but not the easiest.

The adjustment included anger and crying—Mom and I—but we got through it. Now almost a year later, I have come to a hard-to-admit realization: I am my mother's daughter, and not just by physical resemblance.

It is not my father's sense of humor I inherited, it's hers. She is still quick with a quip, takes teasing fairly well, and we laugh together about getting older. My mother can be compassionate and supportive. I try to mimic her sense of style, but not her sense of entitlement, that's not me. It's been challenging, but I have found a new respect for my feisty little Mom, and I like and admire the old woman she has become.

As she was getting ready for bed the other night, she looked up at me and said, "Did you know you are a pretty woman?" "Not pretty, Mom," I replied, "cute, I've never considered myself pretty." "Well you should," my mother replied, "and it should give you confidence as you move about in the world. It's important to recognize who you are." "OK, Mom," I replied, wondering to myself what messages I had incorporated earlier in my life that made me feel like I didn't measure up to her expectations, not even when I became a mother myself. "I was hoping for a little girl," my mother replied when we called to announce the birth of our first, and it turns out, only child, a little boy.

Did I imagine those words? It's been 41 years since my son was born. Was there a context surrounding the words that I've forgotten? Why did I grow up thinking I was so much less, when my mother now tells me that I am so much more?

Now our roles are somewhat reversed, so I guess I will never know—but that's okay. Mom is showing me how to get through old age, and I am doing my best. And if Mom ever asks for gingerbread cookies, I know where to buy the best ones in town!

Susan Einhorn

Share the joy and gift of your work. It will enrich all who hear it.

EXERCISE:

Take a few deep breaths and relax. Focus on the breath. Imagine entering your childhood home.

What does your house or apartment look like? Is it dark or filled with light? Are there fresh flowers and plants?

Is it musty or clean and fragrant in the hallway, in the living room, the bedrooms?

Is it like a museum or furnished with broken furniture? Comfortable and approachable or filled with plastic and synthetic fibers?

Is the kitchen filled with warm and welcoming aromas? Are the cupboards bare?

Revisit your childhood home with the eyes and heart of a child and the mind of an adult. Remember that the past is not real. It only has the power you assign it.

Allow a specific scene that took place in your home to surface. Take the first one you become aware of remembering. Write the scene including details, people, and conversations. If a specific circumstance does not surface, just write the physical description. Often, a scene will surface as you describe and recall physical specifics.

The past sheds light on the present. It helps you decide how to live in the future. Viewing the past with adult eyes allows the release of childhood. It also puts you in touch with happiness and love. Many wounds imprison because of the psychic albums in which they are kept. When you write about such things give permission for the *re-framing* of events or incidents. You can transform how these experiences are held. The realigning of painful, destructive memories allows for liberation and emotional adjustment. Become healed of the poison of regret; release from the anger that stays lodged in a hip, shoulder or heart.

I had a custom-made, mahogany dresser in my childhood bedroom. My mother was allergic to imperfections; at some point every day she'd be in my room checking the furniture as if she were checking an addict's arm for needle marks. She spent more time attending to the dresser than to me, her child.

The piece of furniture outlived her. It's in my basement. Its drawers are cedar-lined. I keep out-of-season clothes in it. I never could bring myself to use it for either of my daughters; every time I looked at it I felt the same neglect I had experienced as a child.

One day I allowed myself to write about it and all sorts of young emotions flew out on to the page. But through the process of writing I was able to witness my mother; I saw her lavishing care on an object and saw how the action stemmed from her own sense of deprivation. She had gone through the Depression thinking that she would never be able to own special and valuable things and she was someone to whom aesthetics mattered. I was suddenly able to understand a part of her and let go of some of the emptiness I felt. Now, when I'm putting away the out-of-season clothes, the veneer of neurosis is gone and in its place is appreciation.

Expect to be happy. We are the totality of the stories we tell ourselves. You will rise to the level of your own expectations.

Genuine healing is revealed through the acceptance of any situation while being authentic and learning to be serene.

AFFIRMATIONS:

I permit my flow into wholeness and let right action flow through me.

SUMMARY:

- Healing comes with compassion.
- Forgiveness comes with patience.
- Trust that writing eventually brings serenity.
- Radiate love both inwards and out into the world; no matter what is going on in life this has an amazing effect.
- Genuine healing is revealed through authentic acceptance of any situation.

CHAPTER FOUR:

CHANGE THE CHANNEL

The Practice of Supportive Programming

There are more things in Heaven and Earth than are thought of in our philosophy.
— William Shakespeare
Hamlet

Needless to say, when Hamlet spoke these words he was a troubled soul. The contemplative prince of Denmark had suddenly found his father's untimely death thrust upon him and that was just the *beginning* of the poor fellow's troubles! A sense of overwhelming alienation and guilt, duty and hypocrisy enveloped him in fog while procrastination, his tragic flaw, plagued him unmercifully.

How different it might have all been had he sought the support that *writing* about a predicament can bring. His exquisite mind could have led to action and healing, rather than emotional paralysis and destruction. Self-loathing and doubt prevented him from accessing the skills needed for coping. Writing the issues out would have brought unimagined clarity; he could have ruled well and eventually achieved happiness.

While going through a crisis or confronting the melancholy of unresolved situations, many would find themselves in a haze. Fear can cloud perspective and prevent acceptance of what needs to be done. Feeling overwhelmed has much of society today resorting to familiar, weak habits. Momentary comfort might be found before self-disgust kicks in. There may also be an unconscious investment in staying stuck. As always, bringing compassion and courage to this journey leads to healing. Learning to lean on the strength of writing provides needed solutions.

Through writing it is easier to discover what is motivating or crippling, healthy, or destructive. It is then a relief to see the stagnation for what it is and detach from the potent emotions which perpetuate dis-ease. Usually this does not happen overnight.

It is scary to go into uncharted waters, especially if going against family patterns (even if they are dysfunctional). Repetition of the familiar *is* comforting. To change requires a willingness to take responsibility and endure temporary discomfort; dealing with life's struggles the same way as always, consistently produces the same results.

Writing pointedly shows how familiar patterns provide immediate gratification usually craved when all else requires discipline and strength, especially during trying times. When we feel depleted it is natural to want to succumb to what is easy (think of how people who have almost drowned report the seductive comfort of just 'giving in').

The writing process teaches transcendence of emotion. By observing what is written with a sleuth's curiosity, many mysteries can be solved. When writing with passion and honesty it is possible to observe and appreciate feelings but not be governed by them.

Name three to five weak patterns or habits which bring immediate relief from frustration, fear or other normal, yet unproductive feelings. These habits could be anything from emotional eating (chocolate and carbs head the list) to an overabundance of sleep, alcohol, reality TV, withdrawal from friends, or an inability to be alone during stressful times:

1. ______________________________

______________________________.

2. ______________________________

______________________________.

3. ______________________________

______________________________.

4. ______________________________

______________________________.

5. ______________________________

______________________________.

Now write about how these habits are truly self-defeating. Notice, you are not being asked to change any behavior, just to become aware of it.

____

____

____

____

____.

Patterns are also like muscles; they atrophy from disuse, so keep exercising the new ones, making them vibrant and strong. You must be vigilant as the old habits always lie in wait, looking for a chance to take hold again. Become aware of the new habit; this leads to repeated reward and the desire for repetition.

Remember that writing brings awareness of thought and action; awareness is the key to adjusting. At first, you begin to notice the negative *after* it has occurred. Who amongst us have not eaten a doughnut, had an extra drink or lost our temper and regretted it immediately afterwards? Stay vigilant and begin to notice *as* you are in the process of transgressing. Over time if the motivation for change is strong, awareness will support the alteration of action *before* doing something unproductive. Writing brings ease and compassion to this work. It allows us to slow down and lead an examined life, correcting and improving as we proceed.

When feeling lost, locate the trail that journaling provides. What do you need to do in order for this to work? Just have the *willingness*—be open to having faith that this will work. Agree to suspend doubt and hopelessness.

You will learn to think more clearly and rationally as you ramble and vent on to the non-judgmental page. Fear expressed in words seems smaller, more manageable and no longer controlling. By unloading your bogeymen (or women) you are able to literally lighten the load and perhaps see a logical course of action. If you are someone who thinks that you must always do something to ameliorate a situation, you might discover that sometimes it is best to do nothing.

Remember: Creating new patterns will not magically make old ones go away. Childhood scars and old pathways may never fully disappear. However, they can fade unseen by everyone except the most critically observant. By writing regularly you train yourself to observe and appreciate new, healthy pathways, which will starve out the old ones.

Write about issues or record daily thoughts and behaviors which heighten your awareness of and appreciation for the process.

EXERCISE:

Close your eyes and imagine that you are staying in a rustic, charming, seaside cottage. You've just had a delicious repast of fresh fish, vegetables and fruit. The dishes are clean, the chores are done. Inhale as you are gently led to a beach right outside the door. Exhale as illness, loss, and anguish are taken from you. Inhale and settle down on the softest deck chair imaginable. Exhale.

Inhale the gentle sea air and feel the warmth of the sun as it envelopes you. Become aware of your senses being heightened. Listen to the sea gulls and the tide gently kissing the shore. Exhale.

Feel the salt air caress your shoulders as muscles relax. Know that this is what heaven must be like.

As you are enjoying this visualization notice a small grayish cloud on the horizon. It is your fear. It does not alarm or affect you as you see it apart from yourself and are very much aware of how small it is in relation to the entire vista. What is this cloud composed of? What is contained within? Breathe.

What shape is the cloud? What is its color and size? Breathe. Take a moment and see yourself rushing to batter down the hatches against the effects of fear. If you are in the habit of anticipating the worst, let the fear speak to you. Direct your inner wisdom to answer it. Calm yourself with dialogue.

When you are ready slowly open your eyes and let yourself express all that this fear is trying to tell you.

Exercise:

Close your eyes once more. Imagine the fear in physical form again. Imagine a vault, wall-safe, or file cabinet with a lock. Visualize the fear shrinking into manageable size. Lift it and place it within one of these containers. Allow yourself to lock it away. Open your eyes once more and write about this.

Another version of this is to continue breathing as you progressively imagine the fear's changing color, shape, and size. For instance, at first you may see a bright red square that is as big as a cave. During the next round the shape may change, the color may fade and the size could shrink. Each time you visualize, the fear may morph into different, less vivid forms. With practice, the fear actually evaporates. Record your thoughts and feelings about this. Know that you can return to these visualizations and insights whenever you feel overwhelmed or frightened.

When used in conjunction with therapy, writing allows you to identify various voices and concerns. How to know if you are on the right path? Feelings let you know. If you write truthfully and do *not* experience a sense of relief or satisfaction, you are on the wrong track. Feeling rewarded, fulfilled, relieved or satisfied is the aim. Of course, when going through a life-altering time, one session of writing might not bring instant relief. Be patient and diligent; trust the process and a guaranteed moment will emerge. An *aha!* moment is one of sheer revelation, when everything comes together, when it all makes sense and brings meaning to reality, no matter how difficult the circumstances.

Remember: What happens in our earlier lives affects the way we deal with trauma now. If we didn't mourn a loss completely, we carry it with us, all the time. We will unconsciously respond to current pain as if experiencing the original–almost reliving the emotions unconsciously. The new pain will trigger past losses unless processed in a healthy complete way, such as writing provides.

We may never get *over* tragic losses but we can get past them, learning to tolerate strong feelings, letting them go without resorting to old numbing comforts. Of course this is easier said than done. Desire, patience and determination are essential.

According to Wayne Dwyer, the renowned motivational leader, we must coax poisonous, lazy, dysfunctional, nonproductive thoughts and habits down the stairs, one at a time, dragging them to the curb. Being in denial or drowning our sorrows is toxic. Cleaning our inner houses or changing the channel in our minds is healthy.

Affirmations are like the clean, clear water that is poured in the jar to create healthier self-talk. Whatever crisis or dilemma you are now facing is handled with the more mature, intelligent, stronger voice. Combined with periods of focused, triggered writing affirmations promote fluidity, eventually clearing the murkiness of whatever is still clouding happiness.

If in your writing you unearth seminal experiences of being told as a child that you were clumsy and incompetent (or other criticisms), writing about it now will allow the exorcising of whatever ghosts still haunt you.

When ghosts depart, you may experience feelings of emptiness. This too can seem daunting. For instance, writing your way to awareness about a dysfunctional relationship might bring up anxiety about being alone. You must nurture yourself with the knowledge that you will then have room to heal core issues. It is when you are willing to be with this void that meaningful answers can be found and lasting fulfillment manifested.

Learning to be dedicated to the writing takes practice, especially if you suffer from approach-avoidance. Muster the energy to drag yourself to the writing table until your sensitivity to the benefits deepens. Reward yourself after having written. Physical exercise energizes but until you commit there is usually resistance. Listen only to the voice within that is positive and motivating. Ask the other, needy, indulgent self to wait—or better, just don't talk to it at all! You may feel so much better that without being cajoled you find yourself simply making the time needed, and even wanting to increase the duration of each session. This is a sure sign that transformation is underway.

EXERCISE: *Clustering*

We could all use a little help when confronting something new.

This is an easy exercise that is used widely in schools as it aligns itself with releasing the conscious, left brain. This, once again, accesses our creative, unconscious voice.

The method is called *clustering*, and like everything else in this book, it can act as the imagination's jumpstart. Simply start by writing down one word and circling it without lifting your pen from the page.

Before you are finished circling, another word will find its way to the surface and write itself. The words you write don't have to be connected, but often are. The connection may not be obvious but afterwards a hint, a clue, a sign of what is going on under the surface is usually revealed.

For instance, if you use the word CONFUSION to begin, your paper might look like this:

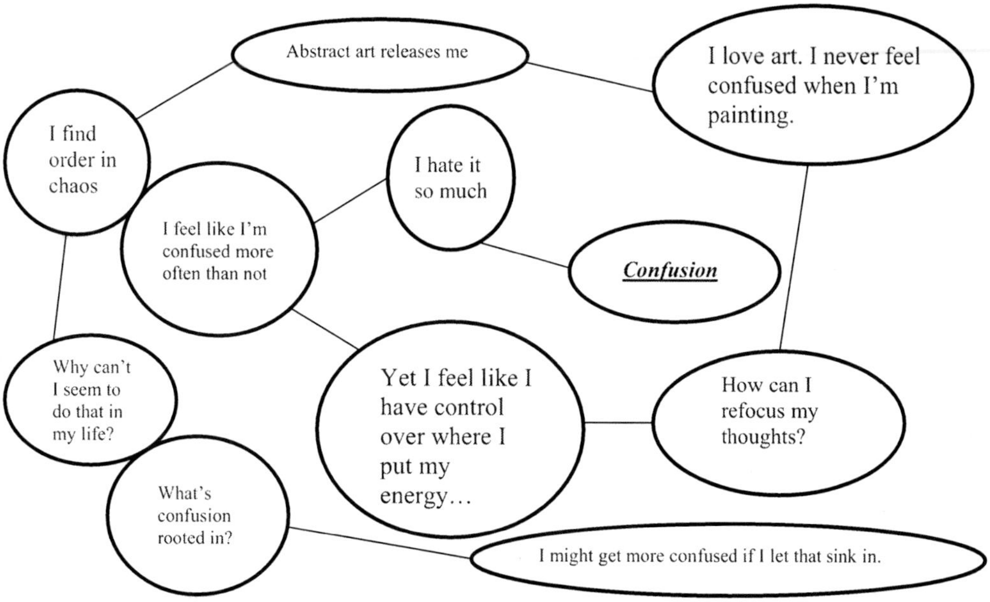

Allow yourself freedom, have fun. Play around. Think of a season. For example, if you are doing this exercise in the winter, write the word WINTER on the page and circle it, then skate along the page, releasing connected words on to the paper. Then give yourself a prompt to write, such as:

As I sit in the coldest time of the year and think of the future, I am on the brink of newness—frozen parts of me come to the surface, crystallizing new thoughts, new ideas and buried memories.

Winter is the season to go inward, to allow plans, inspiration and motivation to ignite the fuel of our being. A time to hibernate and snuggle, to burrow in. Light a fire in the hearth and allow the burning of the old, the releasing of toxins, watching as they burn and crackle; you are then left warmed, rested and ready for spring.

Apply this concept to whatever season finds you reading this.

Ask Yourself:

What does spring feel like? ______________________________

What color does it bring to mind? ______________________________

What smell? ______________________________

What does it feel like when I touch it? ______________________________

What activities does it bring to mind? ______________________________

What personal issue relates to this season? ______________________________

How can this information be used for my healing? ______________________________

The first step to life transformation is to see what is; that *is*, to acknowledge where you are right now. Be moderate in your expectations. Do not push the outer edges. Extend your timeline to accomplish goals at a reasonable pace. While doing physical exercise you need to stretch slowly at first and not stress tight muscles, so you must learn to slowly breathe into any change and carefully press the reset button. The last thing we want is an addiction to being perfect. If this *is* an issue Marion Woodman's **Addiction to Perfection** (Inner City Books, Toronto 1982.) is an excellent book on the dangers of this subject.

EXERCISE:

Close your eyes and take a long, deep gentle inhale.

Release.
As you take the next few breaths notice if your mind is chattering. If it is, allow yourself to repeat the word *'So'*, on each inhale and *'Hum'*, on the exhale. Repetition of these Sanskrit sounds releases chatter. Focus and release.

Feel your feet planted firmly on the ground. Let go of any negative thoughts you may be aware of harboring.

Inhale the word WILLING. Give yourself permission to let go.

What will replace the negative… can you see yourself feeling content, for instance? Give yourself permission to be immersed in peace. What does this feel like?

Allow your mind to drift to a current frustrating situation or emotion. This could be anything from feeling rage or resentment to seeking indulgence. Ask yourself if there is some benefit you get from being this way. See if you can recall where in your past you picked up this pattern, is it related to some event in your childhood, some betrayal, slight or bullying?

Are you willing to look at a childhood wound, as if watching it on a screen, without judgment? If so, open your eyes and begin to describe what you have seen. If not, ask what is in the way. If it is too painful to recall a loss and its subsequent feelings, remind yourself that once you release the pain on the page it will no longer have such a hold or produce the patterned response. Remind yourself that the events are no longer real. Breathe.

If not connecting with your current upset then describe in detail what the pain is, without censoring yourself. Whichever situation you choose to describe, come back into the room and begin to write, non-stop for the full twenty minutes.

After writing, return to conscious, closed-eye breathing. Visualize the pain of this memory rinsing down a drain. You may still want to hold the memory, but the pain will be lessened or disappear totally. One of the writers mentioned earlier, says that she always receives clarity and comfort from what she writes:

SURFING

I'm not willing to let go
I'm clinging to my pain
Don't want to have compassion
I'm pouring like the rain

I'm gushing like a fountain
Spurting up and out with force
Fuelled by rejection
My anger at the source

Observe your thoughts he said
But don't believe they're true
My feelings now are sticking
To my gut like Superglue

I'm riding out the feelings
Like surfing on a wave
I feel the motion under me
But my surfboard won't behave

I can observe my anger
There's frustration at the core
Disappointment underpins me
And I'm vulnerable and raw

Where is the resolution
Of this cresting wave I ride
Can pain like this be healed
If that's what I decide

Forgiveness lies beneath me
On the sandy ocean floor
But the storms of deeper feelings
Bring me back to taste much more

The air is cool and salty
As I'm riding out this wave
And I'm breaking into droplets
When I blow apart this rage

Perhaps it'll all blow over
And a calmer tide appear
The ocean is more powerful
Than this overwhelming fear

Ruth Netter

Sometimes when I feel overwhelmed I force myself to go outside and look at the night sky. The enormity of it gives me perspective; it reminds me that as I am a small part of something larger, my problems are just a small part of me, they are not *who* I am. I find this simple observation to be extremely powerful. It immediately reminds me of the moment when I first realized how miniscule my problems were in the larger scheme of things. One glance at the night sky is the impetus needed for me to calm down and redirect my perspective.

Remember when you were a child and birthdays held such fascination? Remember when you thought that anything was possible and you were ignorant of depression, angst, addictive thinking and the like? Let yourself return to that innocence for a part of every day; let the re-creation lift you above what you are contending with now.

Exercise:

Close your eyes and breathe gently as you recall a favorite birthday. It may be conjured up from a memory or a photo. It may consist of pieces from various birthdays. Allow yourself to recreate pleasant moments, presents received and wishes fulfilled.

Imagine sitting in front of the most beautiful cake, in present time. Check in with yourself and see how you feel. Make a wish for your future. Breathe in, and as you exhale blow out all the candles for your wish to come true. See it happening. It is beneficial to retain, and come back to, the feelings you have around this wish.

As you open your eyes leave cynicism, disbelief, and disappointment alone for now. Reconnect with the delight of childhood and the belief that you can wish your desires into being. Tinkerbell asked all of us to clap our hands if we believed. Believe that whatever you are dealing with will pass. Believe that you will reconnect again. Believe in yourself. Believe in the healing power of nature and the support of others. Believe in a higher power. Believe in the transitory nature of problems and realize that you are much more.

This is extremely challenging during difficult times. If you find an obstacle to believing positive things in general then utilize the idea of being *willing* to believe. As mentioned in Chapter One, healing and wishing cannot prevent someone from dying, or bring about the return of loved-ones but it can strengthen us to deal with our circumstances and therefore be healed of the utter pain. Keep coming back to the willingness and watch your wishes start to come true.

The Caretaker:

At some point in life we might have to face being a caregiver to someone else. The responsibility of it often collapses into burden. There is a psychological phenomenon called *caretaker stress*. When members of a family are seriously ill, the one who is left with most of the responsibility often neglects herself. Caretakers need to acknowledge the additional stress load they have taken on. Relief can be experienced as a result of writing about the issues and people involved. Patience is required. This usually does not occur in one sitting.

In America never before have there been so many choices, or demands on our time. Women today expect themselves to do it all and do it gracefully. We usually leave little time for ourselves. We must find comfort by taking extreme self-care. Yoga, meditation or just conscious breathing in the parking lot or subway will work. A child's smile, a massage, prayer, a new lipstick or scarf; whatever small joy we can permit is essential during periods of overload.

Even with all these practices we may be too embarrassed, ashamed or unaware that we are suppressing unattractive, judgmental thoughts and feelings. If we remember that it is fine to feel *anything*, we lighten the load.

Eileen was suffering from cancer and was the mother of a frisky sixteen year-old as well as caretaker to her ailing father. She was exhausted, and found herself feeling guilty and challenged. She realized that her husband was afraid of losing her and behaving strangely but she had no patience for his emotional absence. She noticed that she was angry most of the time. In fact she was furious. Through meditation on the page she came to realize that she had been outwardly focused on trying to manage her daughter, husband, and father instead of caring for her self.

Over the next few months of writing, she found that the more she gave to herself, the calmer she became and more skilled as a parent and spouse. Her daughter and husband gained new respect for her as she learned to honor herself.

EXERCISE:

Allow yourself to imagine coming to a place of meditation in an ocean, or any other natural sea. This time imagine the golden tip of your tailbone swishing out from your body as if it was the tail of the most exquisitely colored fish, undulating its way through life. Inhale. Joyfully swim amongst the coral reefs. Breathe, feeling the nutrients in the water feeding your every cell.

Quiet your mind and drift to a place where all is harmonious. Breathe. What has to be going on for this to happen? What are you surrounded by, who is there for you? Do you need to distance yourself from anyone?

Consciously register this feeling of peace. Know that you can come back to this place whenever you choose. Now slowly open your eyes and focus on the paper in front of you. Describe, in detail, what the feeling of wellness, of being 'in-tune' with your self, is like.

Feel free to use similes or metaphors to compare unusual connections. By opening up to comparisons you are activating the creative part of your brain. Your writing becomes visual and you will be more able to remember the images.

Remember: a simile compares two things using the words *like* or *as*, such as I feel as peaceful *as* a Tibetan monk at morning prayers.

I feel *as if* I have just slept one hundred years. I am *like* a bride as I radiate love.

After a relaxing bath, I smell *as* sweet as honeysuckle growing wildly by the river.

Metaphors embody the comparison: I am a Madonna; still, compassionate, and serene. I am renewed, an infant unattached to stress and hardship.

Both options create a picture in your mind. They give us an instant snap-shot to return to while stressed.

A simile: ____.

A metaphor: ____.

Have fun with this. Be conscious of how you feel a shift in perspective as you play.

When going through times of unusual stress, we often forget to have fun. We lose our balance and can even forget *how* to enjoy ourselves, often feeling undeserving if those close to us are suffering.

It is imperative that we provide ourselves with some healthy, good-old enjoyment for a part of every day, no matter what.

Post Traumatic Stress Syndrome

They used to call it shell-shock. I believe that we are all suffering from this, to one degree or another because of the times in which we live. It is necessary to address this as it interferes with our functioning, sometimes to an extreme degree.

Telling your story, whether to loved-ones, unknown readers, or yourself, allows you to turn your life into works of art; all great works of literature tell stories of human struggle and suffering. We each have a rich, deeply textured life; knowing this should make everything more tolerable.

EXERCISE:

Breathe…Take an aspect of your care-giving and write it as a story happening to someone else. Be as objective as you can. Locate an area in your care-giving or other area of life that calls for an adjustment. You know to bring your car to the mechanic for a re-alignment… don't *you* deserve the same care? Writing helps assess and analyze where adjustment and refocusing are needed.

Sometimes being grief-stricken, lost, or disappointed is the appropriate way to feel. The trick is to allow the emotions without judging or attaching to them. You don't need to adjust your feelings…just your reactions to them.

If you find yourself struggling, the Buddhists say to learn to love the struggle. It is a sign of growth, of change. Learn to thank the struggle for coming into your life to teach important lessons. Here are some comments from a student grappling with anger at having to deal with life's issues:

> *Anger feels like a wicked infection; a serious staph infection—where the rubbery core center in the middle of red, swollen skin—looks like a yellow worm—wriggling, carrying the infection through my blood, intertwines it with each fiber and vessel. Anger, like the worst of infections sears itself in my spine and my bones where no antibiotic can reach even with long needles and pick lines that dump into a chamber of my heart. Anger can take over your soul so completely that you become angry at yourself for being angry that you couldn't stop it, that you felt it like any human would, that you couldn't avoid it, that you're not perfect in vision and deed, that you are powerless against it because you can't stop it. Anger sweeps over you like a riptide and it cycles like the tide. So you eat and otherwise try to*

hide and bury your head even as the infection spreads and seethes in the substances in which I seek to drown them—the mediums of self abuse are all sustenance for anger.

How do you step away from anger when you are angry? Maybe you can't step away, maybe you can only lay there, transfixed by nausea and the fever of the burning red-faced shame, maybe you can only try to fly away on wings you don't have or on the wind currents of acceptance or the laughter where we can remember for a moment that control is an illusive, that maybe there is no rational reason why this happened, that we are still as whole as we believe ourselves to be.

Anger has hurt me because it has made me more self-destructive than the object of my anger ever could. The shame of being shamed, the powerlessness of losing power you never had. Anger has been my worse enemy.

My own anger at my anger ratcheted the pain up so high I have to surrender, like those men in the Civil War who passed out as their legs were sawed off, the bullet falling sideway from their mouths and their teeth cracked and broken. Biting the bullet, finally spitting it out—I am learning to say 'enough'.

Loretta Cummings

If we allow ourselves to go deep within, to sit quietly and write it out, answers will be revealed. Sometimes being disgusted works too. The mind doesn't know whether we are positively or negatively motivated—whatever gets us to make appropriate adjustments works. Writing can be like a chiropractic treatment, a release, not unlike a massage.

In her book, **The Courage to be Brilliant**, Marta Monahan (Los Angeles, Vittorio Media:1999.) describes how the eagle, the only bird that is able to correct his flight when off-course, teaches us to adjust our flight ever so slightly, to hit our target, to reach our goal. Writing reveals where we are off-course and helps us aim, once more.

Jessica was a graduate student at the age of fifty two, and was suffering from depression. She had successfully raised her four boys and assisted her husband in his career. Everyone assumed that this was why she had put off finishing her doctoral thesis. But that wasn't it. She had been close to completing but couldn't take the last few steps. Frustrated, and so tired of procrastinating, she was now ill and depressed. The doctors didn't know what was wrong, but she did. She had used her family as an excuse, she admitted. Now that her family was self sufficient, she felt despondent. An intelligent and worldly woman, she tried changing her diet, talking to friends, exercising more and praying. She finally took herself to the doctor who prescribed light, short term medication, coupled with therapy.

After six months and six visits the doctor proclaimed "You are torturing yourself with this degree. Maybe you really don't want it." "I do," wailed Jessica, usually very poised and in control. "Well," the doctor said "I will give you medication for two more months. If the rough draft of your thesis isn't done by then you must agree to let it go. Agreed?" Jessica wrote in class the next week; "Something fired up in my brain hearing the ultimatum. I was excited by the challenge. I'll show her, I thought."

In our writing session she recalled being taunted for being afraid as a child. She was always the last one on the diving board at camp. Everyone in her ten year old group would walk up and dive. They snickered as she took her turn and stopped. "Jessica isn't ready."

"It's ok," her counselor told them. "Maybe tomorrow, Jessica. Let's go to lunch." Jessica now wrote how she then jumped into the freezing water. She wanted to show everyone that she had what it took—that she was ready.

Recalling this in class brought tears to Jessica's eyes. I hadn't remembered that incident until we began to write about a childhood challenge. "If I handled that when I was a puny, scared child, I can finish my thesis, also," she realized. "I can meet this challenge. I am ready. I guess I've always only done things after a dare. I don't know why and I don't care: I'm just going to do it."

By allowing herself to own up to the struggle, Jessica discovered her motivational switch. Remember, it doesn't have to be positive... whatever unlocks the door, whatever gets us past the threshold.

Another student of mine, Meredith, realized, *Emotional stimuli, like witnessing a daughter breaking up with her beau, has often plugged me into all my dysfunctions (bad parenting, tumultuous marriage, setting a poor example, blah, blah, blah). I backslide, reverting to poor habits once more. When I am able to write and articulate what happens with that tape in my mind and how it plays out for its duration, I am cleansed and ready to get back to the programming the next day. It is a challenge to stay hopeful, to have faith, at times like this. That obsessive, all or nothing personality prevents me from knowing that the occurrences trigger remnants of the way things used to be; thankfully those periods are short and far between, at this point.*

Know that these periods may still come but they also definitely go.

Ask yourself: **What is Holding Me Back?**

Being stuck is common; but painful. We can lose a sense of what we've accomplished and who we have become. We settle. Feelings of shame compel us to justify everything with excuses. In the beginning we may be unaware of our situation. Awareness makes us ashamed and the vicious cycle of excuse keeps us paralyzed. Once again, we can write our way out of this, or any, box. Our intuition knows the truth about us, but like a princess imprisoned by the nasty queen, we languish. Instead of waiting to be rescued we need only to unlock our own intuitive wisdom. Writing does this.

EXERCISE:

Take a seat, placing your feet squarely on the floor, hands in lap. Breathe in through your nose...allow the breath to focus on the two points of your shoulder blades as you squeeze them toward each other. Breathe in down your spine, center your tailbone and anchor it.

Become aware of your heart opening up. Breathe in, filling the heart, retracting and lifting the stomach and pelvis, anchoring the tailbone. Imagine your shoulder blades becoming wings, unfurling. Breathe in, knowing that your spirit is now able to fly. You are safe to freely reflect on the pain you have been living with. Locate a place within where you feel confused or hopeless and let it speak.

Now slowly come back into the room.

What have you just seen and experienced? Describe any vision or experience you may have had.

Each person's memory holds the story of us all. Today, women came to class with concerns, complaints and complexities. It was no different than any other class. We are always working on issues.

According to Sarah Ban Breathnach, in **Daybook of Abundance**, we whine because it relieves us of our burdens. We complain because it releases the pressure cooker in our brains. We sigh so that we don't scream. But read what letting it out artistically sounds like and where the writing took this writer:

Selfish Selfish Selfish Selfish so selfish very selfish extremely selfish unusually selfish absolutely selfish self-satisfied self-involved self-centered self-contained and then what? Without self without the inner the outer the externally shattered mixed up mantra preying mantis self-indulged inter-woven unusually ungiving unnurturing outstandingly intentionally voraciously ferociously intensely uncontrollably unconditionally self-centeredly all about me whining childish child crying & screaming, mewling & puking in a Shakespearean sonnet send in the clowns rolling and tumbling pulling and pushing thirty three striped leggings Punch & Judies through the roof of the tiny red car they emerge unscathed and happy large red smiles black star eyes white glistening teeth staring mockingly back at the entranced enchanted audience they snicker at us waiting for our applause our cotton candied slurpy hands clap for hours no days we hurt the palms of our hands we clap too hard and the clowns fall down roll to the side of the stage keep rolling over and over move over rolling further and further over until there is no room anywhere no room no room the Mad Hatter said move over you bitch get outta here you all about me it ends right now but I am selfless and I am no longer keeping you on my list the long long list the neverending words that I say each day the ones I hear the little words the tiny little meaningless words that screech and moan as I writhe, twist, turn, spin, dance, yell, contorting into small microcosmic pieces of clay and flesh I spin forever into dark spirals enunciating words that no one enunciate them well and even I don't know what they mean another language another time, place, moment in timespace emerging through the crowded cloud I smile forever never giving up or allowing myself to fall I will never become a bird but I may sing like one.

Ginger Hendler

If you write it all out, whether in letters to God, your mother, aunts, friends, or ancestors, you can feel curiously renewed, fortified and comforted. When kept inside, it has the power to make you ill.

For some, there is a fear of the void created when not complaining. What will fill the time? What will the focus be? Where will the intrigue and drama be found? What will be talked about with others? Will there be relief any other way than having the situation validated as horrid?

I remember long ago hearing the axiom that really small minds talk about other people, middling minds talk about things and larger minds discuss ideas. Oh, how many of us struggle with this one!

None of this is to belittle our concerns, whether real or imaginary, but let us use the tool of writing to anchor us as we find our way. Without our own counsel, and its ability to heal, we would be rudderless in any storm.

Ask yourself how badly you want change. How much psychic pain can you stand? If you've had enough and are tired of torturing yourself (even indecision is a form of torture, no matter how subtle), be honest and state what is really important to you. If it's peace of mind, for instance, you need to make achieving it the priority for the day. This might mean writing, or doing yoga, as soon as you wake up.

There is an old illustration of this that has been going around the self improvement circuit for years. No one seems to know who to credit for first thinking of it–otherwise I would pay homage. Here it is:

If you have a large jar and need to fit in ten large rocks (your priorities), fifteen small stones (things that are important but not essential) and a cup of sand (all life's little chores, errands, pleasantries and extras), what would you put in first? If you choose the sand, you wouldn't have room for the rocks and stones. Except for breathing, food, shelter, and taking care of dependents, everything else can wait.

First do your heart's directive (exercise, spiritual practice, your writing) and then fit everything else around that. By changing this channel you will find yourself with more energy, increased drive, a healthy outlook and less anger.

For the people who are battling cancer, as are the students at Gilda's Club, it is imperative that they be honest about all of their feelings, especially anger. There is often guilt and shame attached to this. Some students may be drowning in "Why me?"

We are hungry. We're haunted by the need, the wish or the desire to unburden, unload, break through, empty out, create, express and be joyful. We pretend that we're o.k. but we're not. It's too much. Are we willing to let go? Are we willing to really have it all—to have everything that truly matters and to finally let go of the rest? Many of us are so pent up, angry, wounded and defended by what has strangely become everyday life that we can't fully breathe and just be. But we must. It is imperative to breathe. Writing is like breathing on to a page. Obviously, without breathing we cease to exist. Not expressing what is inside erases us, also.

When It Doesn't Work

Iris was extremely upset about the way her brother and two sisters were not taking enough responsibility in caring for their senile mother. Iris was the oldest and a doctor, a natural caregiver. Although she was totally willing to manage the bulk of the work, her siblings' lack of concern irritated her. It bothered her sense of ethics. Through her writing we hoped that she would release her attachment and judgment. However, she was not willing to let go of her anger and self-righteousness. No matter how many times she wrote about the situation she stayed stuck. She finally stopped coming to class.

Unless we are willing to let go, we block the road to consciousness. Unfortunately, Iris continued to suffer for the year following her mother's demise. After mourning by herself, having alienated her siblings, and without the physical activity of caring for her mother, she was finally ready to confront the unrelenting pain. She returned to class and slowly, painstakingly released her anguish, her judgment and most of all, the reluctance to let go of her mom. Holding on to her judgment of the others was keeping the loss of her mother at bay. Only when her pain became so overwhelming and friends found it difficult to continue their support, was she able to begin to resolve it all.

Exercise:

Sit in a comfortable chair or sofa, allowing your feet to touch the floor. Breathe in, from the bottoms of your feet then exhale. Breathe and take in nutrients and minerals; replenish yourself from deep within the earth. Take the breath into your veins and arteries; swirl it all around your heart. Breathe out the back of your head, releasing congestion. Release the muscles in your shoulders, back, waist and thighs. Breathe. Inhale. Exhale negativity, resistance, regret and loss.

Ask yourself if there is anything you are not willing to let go of regarding a particular situation. What feeling do you get from holding on?

Imagine a long beautiful hallway. You are walking towards a door. Take a moment and create the most exquisite, inviting doorway you can conjure up, for you will return here often.

Imagine that once you step over the threshold you will put the burden of *withholding* down. You no longer need to carry it.

Go through the doorway into a chapel. It need not be very big, for only you will come here. It is your sanctuary, where you can let go of everything with ease. You have everything you need. You are content.

There is a pedestal in the center of the room and on it there is a young child. As you approach you see that it is you at age four or five.

Take in the innocence and perfection of this young being. Acknowledge her. In your mind's eye, step back and observe the five primary people who influence and interact with her. Note whether their interactions are mostly (75% or more) positive or negative. Acknowledge what she's been through. Feel her acceptance of everything—feel her absorbing and integrating all that has affected her. What did she have to reject or rebel against in order to save her soul? Notice the strengths and defenses which have formed over time.

Allow yourself to go to her, reach up and take her into your arms. Tell her that she is safe, supported and flows with change. Sit and rock her, telling both selves that it is safe to feel your feelings, that you will not attach to the negative but will allow it to surface and release. Sit for as long as you need to. When you feel ready, allow yourself to come, part-way back into the room and begin to write about all you have just experienced.
Take yourself back into this meeting place as often as possible-once a day if you can, especially when life is challenging.

> *Expect Your Every Question to be Answered,*
> *Expect Your Every Need to be Met.*

Remember that your outcome is directly proportional to your attitude.

In class, an example of what came up from meeting with the Little Girl was from Lore, an extremely attractive, well dressed woman. She was gracious and *seemed* to be at ease. After I asked the women: who is the little girl you, above all, have abandoned? Lore wrote, *I, not my mother, not my father, but I had abandoned her. It was painful to be with her so I left. She has haunted me anyway, clung to me, whines at me and still I don't answer. It has made me ill. Enough! I know how to mother, to nurture, to set boundaries and to deal with consequences, rewards, acknowledgement and support. I know how to love unconditionally—I just haven't done it with myself.* Her tears, at first confounded her. Then, she told us later she felt compassion for what she had endured as a girl. Finally, she broke down, weeping. "I've been carrying this sad waif around my whole adult life. No wonder that I'm always tired. She's been so heavy."

Sylvia, another student, was surprised at what she recorded. *Today is the Beginning; today is the first Day to the Rest of My Life. I am going to have a wonderfully long, enriching life if I start today. Each day I put it off is a day lost forever. I refuse to feel bad for the unfulfilled girl I was but I am now committing to give to her.*

Whatever surfaces during conversations with parts of our selves helps us come back to the place where we are an integrated whole.

As Jessica revisited her child self she allowed those less than positive parts to surface. She realized that she became a liar because her mother would rage at her if she did something wrong. She figured out at a very young age that she had a fifty/fifty chance of avoiding the mother's rage if she lied. She grew up with a tremendous amount of shame surrounding this issue. When she was able to acknowledge and embrace the part of herself that was clever enough to survive she became whole and capable of moving on.

Jessie, an architect in Manhattan who had prided herself for winning prestigious contracts in a field dominated by men, was grappling with her husband's accusations of manipulation.

"I denied his judgment of me for years. Recently, it has threatened the very fabric of our marriage. Honestly, there is nothing that makes me want dissolution. I love Sam and want him to stay. I'm ready to look at the possibility that he may be right."

She chose to explore her childhood. This is what she wrote the first time she did one of the exercises; *I was never given acknowledgement…at least it always felt that way. I learned to fight for it and I fought dirty, if necessary. My mother tried to repress me, squash my spirit with the rigidity of her own. Now I'm loved. I have acceptance. I realize why and how I have habituated that mode of thinking to get my own way at all costs. I am big enough to own up to this little manipulator, this exterminator, and embrace that I was able to keep my spirit alive. I'm willing to heal and love all of me.*

Exercise:

Start by going to your breath. Anchor in the meditative state. Now think of all the different selves you are. A parent? Woman? Little girl? Seductress? Intellectual? Awkward one? Is there an unsavory self from your childhood still being carried, a part that no longer fits? For instance: the liar, the gossiping friend, the unhappy peacekeeper, the cheating student, the judgmental sibling. There could be many more. Spend a moment and see who surfaces.

Imagine a lovely, beige room with seven chairs arranged in a semi-circle. Let each part of you which has just surfaced sit in each of the chairs.

Ask one of the selves to come forward. Ask her why she has stayed with you.

Ask for resolution concerning this issue's manifestation; perhaps it is comfort-eating in times of stress, lying to seem more important than your colleagues, or taking care of others before you care for yourself.

Ask the issue why it is there, how it has served you and whether it is willing to leave. In your mind, move from chair to chair, having each self's voice answer you back.

Who would you, as a friend, be without the unsavory aspect? Love that part of yourself for coping, for helping you survive. Who would you be as a lover? Parent? Student? Victim? Breathe. Finally, in your mind's eye have all the parts integrate back into the whole.

For instance, if you did something unsavory to get ahead at work the Manipulator may truthfully tell you that she was afraid she couldn't get ahead on her own. Teach her to tell herself, "I am so happy and grateful. I will succeed with integrity."

Now write about what took place (for twenty minutes, if possible), what came up and what you can take, leaving the rest to drift away—with your blessing. Over time, you will become aware of these different selves and their needy qualities in written dialogue; feed them with affirmations and appease their longings.

Sandy is what is commonly known as a worry-wart. She was like this whether things were going poorly or well. She had been going through ordeal upon ordeal for approximately two years. Her husband had been diagnosed with cancer. She was widowed once before by the same disease. Her writing work was focused on her sense of fatalism. As she dragged herself to class and sessions with her therapist, she was able to uncover family messages and dictums about negative outcomes and expectations. She went through the process of finally seeing that she could *choose* to focus on something different. Her heart, through her writing, was crying out for compassion. She learned to soothe herself and handle whatever care was needed. After a year of medical treatment, her current husband was declared clear of any cancerous traces. She became painfully aware of how she had worried almost an entire year of her life away.

Worry is a wasted emotion. We worry in our minds and feel the pain in our bodies. We waste precious hours on "what if" when so much never comes to be. If the worst actually does occur we find that we are usually well-equipped to deal with anything, even pain.

Martha had taken her mother into an already overcrowded house. Martha's mother had exhibited signs of dementia and could no longer care for herself. Martha made weekly dinners for the immediate family to bring comfort. Martha held down a demanding job, was also the mother of a learning disabled teenager and wife to a high powered executive. Martha was exhausted.

With the willingness to write out her feelings, she discovered that she had always been afraid to say no. Martha came to class one day complaining that her brother had just requested that his new girlfriend's daughter be included in what was the immediate family's gathering. She reported that she had just tried something we advocate in class:

Ordinarily, this was no big deal but I felt bereft as it was. If she came it meant putting an extra leaf in the table and dealing with another person's energy; it felt like the final piece of straw on my back. In the past I would have acquiesced because that was how I was brought up. I could feel myself becoming physically constricted. I realized that as trivial as it seemed to set another place, I needed that extra energy for me! I called my brother back and gently refused. This was a first and felt stupendous. Remember that we need to take "extreme" measures to make us take notice of ourselves.

Martha began a month-long diet from saying "yes" to everything and everyone. She wrote about her experience with levity and wit. *No one in my family liked me very much, no matter what I did, or said, anyway. Over the years, I realize now, I had set myself up as the punching bag. If I said yes to something they would complain that I didn't do what they had requested fast enough or well enough. So this month I removed the bag and hid the boxing gloves. I gained a new perspective and increased energy as I watched them lunge for me and take swats at the empty air. I was finally able to get it as I watched my brother lean over a little too far, bounce off the ropes and flip outside of the ring. I have more energy and insight now. I realize that I still have work to do – that I'm furious at everyone today. I'm angry that my parents allowed this, that my siblings took advantage and that I set myself up in this role. I hear what we talk about in class and know that I have to forgive all of us and develop compassion for myself as the young girl who saw this as a coping mechanism. I'm just not there yet. I'm just mad…and I'm not going to take it anymore!*

When desperate enough, any one of us can be moved to action, to change. In order to conquer any weak habit takes work. We are complex beings and until core needs are met, there will be no ease.

Giving your self permission to feel, without staying stuck takes willingness, perseverance and, as the beloved psychologist Barbara Schwartz realized, vigilance. Staying tuned to the enlightened, productive, and proven vibration and frequency will allow you to find grace and peace. Vigilance is required to catch any and all negative, wayward thoughts, feelings or actions. They fight hard. They fight dirty. They are fighting for their lives. It is time to starve them out, with mercy, of course.

Activate the positive channel which runs within you, flowing and clear.

Fall in love with this little girl in a way that you may not have been able to before. Begin a life-long relationship where you commit to cherishing her, where you will support and inspire her as you have probably done with others. Find and keep a photo of her on your night table.

EXERCISE:

Close your eyes and breathe the quiet, peaceful breath of childhood. You are safe and warm in your bed. Breathe. It has been a good day. You drift off to sleep dreaming of playtimes of your youth. Breathe. What are you doing? Who are you with? What did you love to do? Play with home-made dough (or Play Dough), climb trees, play doctor, cut paper dolls…

Allow yourself to discover this little girl again now, with loving, adult eyes. Are your desires and needs similar now? Drift for as long as you'd like. Now come back to the present. Take inventory as you now write about one of the memories in the front of your mind.

Did you write about what was particularly pleasing in the activities and hobbies you pursued? Acknowledge what made you unique, how you deserved love then… and still do, now.

Think of how playing brought fun, challenge, and even comfort to you as a child. What aspect of playing with paper dolls for instance, was so appealing? What do you do for pleasure now? Can you cultivate pleasure-giving aspects into your life at present? Might they not give you strength, joy and comfort? Go for what gave you the feeling of joy then. Playing with paper dolls may have brought a sense of creativity or inspiration, which is waiting to be reawakened.

Usually the qualities we enjoyed in childhood play are the same ones that bring us joy now. Whatever brought us happiness then is a key to our authentic selves now.

The pressure of adult living, with all its challenges, often hinders us from being who we truly are.

When you reclaim your authentic self, when she is revealed to you, the release is sometimes overwhelming. If we have often been in a state of anxiety, depression or frustration, possibly we believe that is the real us. We tell ourselves and others that we're just naturally hyper, or anxious. When we become aware of our real, peaceful, calm, cheerful self, we want to let the other go, and it is often scary.

Marie wrote, *this new wretched pain that lives in my arm is the pain of frustration. Frustration at not being able to be who I want to be, the person I know myself to be. The pain is also in a deadly battle with my ego. My ego is fighting for control. It knows that being in control must die and that the battle of fatigue is the stronghold. My eating constantly is my ego wanting to be fed. I want to be nurtured and taken care of. I want to let go—relax, stay in bed, calm down.* Once she saw all this on paper, Marie was able to approach her pain from various angles.

Marie realized that she lived in a state of frustration. Once she became aware of what she had created in order to shield her soft core, she was able to choose something new. She chose self-love and acceptance. She "tuned" herself and was soon spreading a much different energy. Does this always happen with awareness? Heck, no! Many of us choose to continue being in denial, in the throes of excuses, disclaimers and the like. However, if we have the conviction to find peace and fulfillment this work is for us. Human patience, compassion and vigilance are the three graces in this work.

EXERCISE:

Close your eyes and breathe. Listen to the intake of air. Listen to its release.
On each inhale visualize an image of the vibration frequency you want to access. For instance, if you'd like to feel more loved, picture yourself embracing everyone in a way that is open and accepting, no matter what their response. Feel the hum of this energy.

Allow yourself to imagine a color to correspond with the image. When you think of unconditional love, for example, do you see a deep garnet, a cardinal's red robe, perhaps a royal purple or blue? Anchor this. Imagine this color clearing the channel, cleaning out the dysfunctional—let it wash through you. Tell yourself that this color will ground and inspire you every time you see it, whether in reality or in your mind's eye.

Now allow yourself to come partially back to the room you are in and describe what you have seen.

If you read what you have written every morning, and again at night, for at least twenty-one days you will have set yourself to this new, healthier frequency; literally a new channel. You can alter this exercise for a custom fit. If you choose, go get paint chips, a scarf or a flag to jog your connection. If you are more of an auditory person use a sound such as a gong, or whistle, perhaps a wind chime. Whatever it takes to find a higher frequency is worthwhile.

AFFIRMATION:

Today, I am resetting my frequency to one of love, acceptance and compassion for myself and others.

FLEETING LIGHT

Fleeting light
Bedazzled streams
Unconscious patterns
Expansive dreams

Speed is of the essence
Our destination unsure
Running from the past
The future insecure

The journey is inspiring
Mountainous vistas unfold
Rapid transit the vehicle
To a future yet untold

Can we stop a speeding train
When the red light has appeared
A pause to view the landscape
Standing still not all we feared

There's a tunnel in my vision
A dark space just up ahead
And trusting that the light
Will transform my inner dread

Monotonous ambiguity
As seasons change the tide
Frozen lakes and submerged images
That we never really hide

It's a looking glass reflecting
All the weeds that linger there
Without food they cannot flourish
They lie dormant, so beware

But above the frozen river
The sky's a luminous blue
Shift your gaze, and the perspective
Will be transformed anew

When the tracks are so divided
And the future seems to split
Let your engine take a moment
To allow your gears to shift

— Ruth Netter

Breaking the Habit and Curing the Addiction to Feeling Bad

Research is being conducted right now on three divisions of the mind: primal, logical and calm. Obviously we would like to stay in the calm mind as often as we can. This doesn't mean that we won't ever get angry, frustrated, sad or scared. If we are allowing ourselves to feel our feelings without attaching to them then we can even feel disturbing emotions from a calm place. How do we get there when we're somewhere else and lost?

Exercise:

Close your eyes and recall a time (maybe today) when you were feeling agitated or lost; maybe wanted to run and hide. Picture where you'd go—up in a tree, in those clouds, a chasm or in bed with the covers pulled over your head. Breathe.

Imagine being in that lost place once again. You feel like fleeing to the other place where everything and everyone is calm, but don't know how to get there. Breathe.

Watch your mind with gentle acceptance of the situation. Leave the "flight or fight mode" and traverse to a logical, practical place. How did you make the leap?

Breathe.

From your logical, practical mind, allow your *imagination* to come and take logic by the hand; together create a bridge to the other side. Remember each and every detail of what the bridge is built of, where it leads to in that land of calm. Is it built of flowers? Old bricks? High-tech rubber? Recycled paper? This bridge is for you alone. It can appear any time you want to get away to…relaxation and relief.

Breathe. Slowly open your eyes and write about what you saw and felt. Go beyond the description to an imaginary experience. Go as deep within as possible. Remember you can come back to this place often.

Recall some of the affirmations which now crop up automatically. Have you been aware of these new-found thoughts and messages replacing the old negative ones? This will happen more and more if you flood yourself with the positive until eventually most negativity disappears.

AFFIRMATION:

I am totally committed to healthy programming in mind, body and spirit. I always keep my commitments to myself.

SUMMARY:

- Change requires a willingness to be responsible and an endurance of temporary discomfort.
- Dealing with life's struggles the same way as always, eternally produces the same results.
- Pause and slow down through writing; this leads to an enlightened life.
- Have fun, for part of every day, no matter what.
- Free writing provides access to the place where answers are revealed.

CHAPTER FIVE:

RECONDITION

Mastery of Extreme Self Care

Our crowns have been bought and paid for—all we have to do is wear them.
— James Baldwin

As a child, did you hear your parents and others applaud most everything you did? Or did you hear, "Who do you think you are?!" "Can't you do *anything* right?"

Or were you blessed enough to have been with significant adults who did say that anything was possible for you? Did you feel worthy, cared for and approved of?

Healthy self esteem comes from a solid foundation and model of behavior, which provides the necessary tools to successfully deal with crisis and extreme stress.

Many of us are charged with creating that state of self-worth now. There are many voices floating around in our heads besides those of our parents. Athletic coaches, school bullies, religious leaders, relatives, teachers, and partners have all had an impact on who and what we are. If the desire and willingness to examine what we believe about ourselves and our capabilities is present, we can change, and ultimately grow. We are not too old, fed up, far gone, tired, hungry, frustrated, or lonely to grow. A miraculous aspect of being human is that we are adaptable at any age.

Quickly (without forethought) list some of the messages you remember being said about you by those who have been influential in your life. Just write down the first thought that comes:

Mother____

____.

Father ____

____.

Current Partner ____

____.

Past Partner ____

____.

Teacher ____

____.

Coach or Mentor____

____.

Sibling ____

____.

Sibling ____

____.

Children____

____

____.

Neighbor ____

____.

The list could go on and on to include anyone who has ever said anything positive or negative about you. Take these comments, opinions, compliments and criticisms and explore for the next twenty minutes the effect they have had on who you believe yourself to be.

What is your present physical, mental, emotional and spiritual condition? Often during ordeals we are either struggling from moment to moment or busy beating ourselves up for not handling it all. Being kind and acknowledging how well you are actually doing is sustaining and encouraging.

Mentally, I am content to know that I am ______________________________

____.

Physically, I am thankful that ______________________________________

____.

Emotionally, I am pleased that I can call upon my_____________________

____.

Spiritually, I take solace and strength from___________________________

____.

I would like to embrace the following qualities for more success, strength and increased self-esteem (be more compassionate and gentle to yourself, be a do-er not a complainer, etc.):

____

____

____

Love, acknowledgment, and a sense of security are crucial for carrying us through the rough times. How can we be expected to feel safe if as children we didn't have our needs met? Our parents passed on to us the programming they had received. For us to heal and live fully, we must now learn to meet these needs for ourselves in a pro-active way. **Extreme self care** is required!

Awareness and focus are essential for change to occur. I like to think of the phrase **extreme self care** as a magic wand. It helps me to remember that when I am tired, instead of pushing myself, I may need to lie down, have a glass of iced tea or do some yoga stretches instead of heading for the chocolate chips lurking in the back of the freezer. (Truthfully though, some of the time chocolate *is* the only thing that works).

STEP INTO A VISUALIZATION OF WHO YOU WANT TO BE:

What are the things that make you happy, sane and relaxed? These are the ingredients needed for extreme self care. When we are going through times of stress—and I use this word to include grief, trauma, illness and such—we need an extra dose of kindness. We must learn what we need and obtain it; this is a priority!

When programmed with negativity, fear and criticism, it is incredibly challenging to switch the self-talk. If only looking for acknowledgement from others, we will always remain unsatisfied, needy and unfulfilled. We are the only ones who can change what goes on inside us, although the support of others can be a beacon when the way is lost.

Debbie Ford asks her workshop participants what stands in the way of having the most magnificent year of their lives. She asks them to look inside for one thing they are lacking; if they only had this one thing they would have the best year of their lives. When people share what they've identified, such as acknowledgment, she would ask, "Well, do you give that to yourself?"

Did *you* lack positive recognition as a child or adolescent? Read what my student Esther discovered while writing on this issue.

> *As a little girl I was oblivious to 'my place.' I enjoyed each day's sensations and experiences. I loved going to the Chinese restaurant with my family and when my father would invite me to, "Order whatever you'd like," I would eagerly listen to him read the menu. I was about seven or eight the first time I became aware of the insidious look my mother dripped into the IV of my consciousness. I had been listening to the roster of choices, "I'd love the shrimp with the lobster sauce," I blurted. My mother interrupted "Do you have to order the most expensive thing?" Her look read, who do you think you are? Over the next twenty years my mother would ask that question so often to the point that I no longer knew the answer. Of course, now I understand that it was her poverty consciousness; she was unaware that she was infusing me with it, passing on a legacy of self-doubt and scarcity.*

Esther told us that she only became aware of all this when the memory surfaced on the page. When you think of the years and years of programming a person is subjected to since birth, it becomes reasonable to expect that it takes lots of time to have new, healthy habits and thought take hold. It's obviously appropriate to feel sad when experiencing loss, hardship, or illness. But it is what you do with these feelings that determine your future choices.

PATIENCE, FORGIVENESS, VIGILANCE

If you ever learned how to play something such as tennis or the piano, it is obvious how many times it takes to practice each technique. If you learned a few wrong notes, you know it takes twice as long to correct than if you had learned them accurately the first time. The brain reverts back to what is first set up. Be patient and forgive circumstances and yourself for the length of time it now takes to learn new patterns of thought and behavior. See where your strength, compassion and vigilance will lead you.

As adults it is now up to us to supply ourselves with what we didn't get as children. During stressful times we often slip, succumbing to old patterning. I remember that I described it once as tripping off a curb, shrinking to about an inch in height and not being able to climb back up to safety. Now if I find myself overwhelmed, I try to stop and ask if I'm taking extreme self care. I don't remember to do this all the time, unfortunately, but I am becoming more consistent. This allows me to calm down and prevents the mechanism of worrying from starting up.

After years of being in one of my groups, coupled with on-going therapy sessions, Janice wrote me. *I've been known to eat an entire loaf of freshly baked artesian bread (at least it was good quality) but then beat myself up afterwards. It took me years of writing to discover that I was actually plugged into feeling bad. Once I got in touch with this and realized that I was sick of the feeling I was able to channel my emotions more directly into the writing and change what needed to shift. I still like to talk it all out with friends for the feedback and comfort I receive from them but as time goes on and my feeling of dependence on others lessens I am able to find solace and advice from deep within. My writings reveal a level of wisdom that had been there all along but had been clouded over (by false conditioning and stuck feelings). The journey of self-discovery is the most worthwhile experience out there. It is more exhilarating than white water rapid riding and a lot cheaper!*

Carol, an accomplished artist, told the group, "In my adult life I have repeatedly been told that I am too hard on myself. I never knew what people meant by that. Since I started practicing self-acknowledgement, I have been able to relax the impossibly high standard I had set for myself that I was not able to meet, anyway. I spent years perpetuating my lack of accomplishment instead of noticing and appreciating what I *had* done."

What can you acknowledge yourself for handling in any current situation?

____

____

____

____

____.

How could you be taking more care while going through difficult times?

____

____

____.

What would you be doing if you were taking extreme care? Usually I would be slowing down, lowering expectations and resting until I had the energy to address an issue I had been avoiding. As soon as I realize this, even before I take any action, I immediately feel better. Not all better, mind you. This is hard work. Of course, writing it out can speed and deepen the process.

EXERCISE:

Inhale. Imagine standing beneath a gentle waterfall. Watch droplets of water as they reflect the light. Exhale. Now, as you breathe in, notice how the rocks on which you are standing offer firm support. Exhale.

Inhale. Watch how soothing and refreshing the cool water feels on your sun-warmed skin. Exhale. There is nowhere you need to go, nothing you need to do. You can remain here for as long as you'd like. Breathe out the day's stress.

You see a pool a few feet away. Step into the warm, swirling water and feel whatever tension you have been carrying wash away. Imagine a life where you are able to feel this way as often as you'd like.

What qualities and behaviors would living this way include? Would you stretch every morning? Would the mattress you sleep on give the best support scientifically possible? Would the food you'd be eating be organically fresh and full of nutrients? Would meals be eaten at a beautifully set table, and would you treat yourself to flowers or a good book? How much of this do you give yourself now?

Strengthen the vision of how you would like to be. Allow the behaviors which support this way to manifest in your mind. Visualize what extreme self care means for you now. It may be very different from what you had experienced previously in your life. Slowly return to the room. Begin to write and explore many different areas of your life. Have fun with this. Include people, places and things; surround yourself with them. Know that you deserve this.

This vision can become a blueprint to return to every morning or when things become particularly trying. Breathe. Now close your eyes once more. Let your mind drift until you have located a current challenging issue. Allow yourself to review this without attachment.

If a situation surfaces involving other people, conduct an imaginary conversation with them. Take responsibility, without guilt, for your part.

Write about this matter for ten minutes or more, then pause and rest. Now look over what you have written, or come back to it later. Ask: *Have I taken responsibility, without guilt or have I simply blamed others?*

One of the refinements that writing to someone provides is the opportunity to write first and then edit before we send our message. I did this recently with my older daughter, Jeni. We basically have a solid, loving relationship, but we can both be stubborn at times. Recently, we had a momentary breakdown in communication. In the past we would have waited hours, or even a day, before speaking again. This time I wrote a lengthy email, and yet when I revised it, I realized that I had only focused on her behavior. I edited the message, taking responsibility and shifting my perspective before I pressed SEND.

She wrote back lovingly, almost immediately, and we discussed that we both felt a new kind of resolution. The heat of reactive behavior from the past was eliminated, creating room for rational, loving dialogue.

If you can, write a letter to someone now that corrects a misconception, rights a wrong or puts an old issue to rest. There is no requirement for sending the letter. Just the act of writing is healing.

EXERCISE:

Allow yourself to melt into your chair. You are cozy and safe. For the moment, all thoughts of grief, illness, challenge or hardship are put aside. Breathe. Just feel the chair supporting you.

Breathe.
As children we listened to many stories where personification, the giving of human characteristics to inanimate objects, occurred. Dishes ran away with spoons and trees spoke. Now this chair is enveloping you, whispering acknowledgments for all you have done and all that you are, embracing and comforting the inner-child who is in need of the extra hug.

Breathe.

Allow a memory of miscommunication with someone, still alive, or not, to emerge. Play it through your mind as if you were watching a movie. How did you handle the situation? What changes would you make, if you could?

Breathe.

Ask: What things in my life, which no longer serve me, do I need to clear out? What qualities might reveal themselves and blossom?

____

____.

____

____.

What facets of my being do I now want to focus on? What parts do I wish to retain and what new qualities do I now claim?

Tell Yourself:

All I have to do when I am about to fall into the void is breathe. I am safe.

When you are ready, come partially back into the room and write what you've realized.

After writing and reviewing, can you release the pain, fear, confusion and loss? Were you aware of blocking anything? Breathe.

Sit for a while with peace and inner joy.

Learn to accept wherever you are in the process. You cannot put an exact number on how many days, or years, it takes to heal. It is different for everyone. Acceptance of where you are at any given moment during the journey actually accelerates healing. Be aware of strong emotions surfacing.

If you are grieving for someone, or something, remember that it means you have loved deeply. Confusion is sometimes also a natural response, although it can be extremely uncomfortable. Combat fear of the future with self-love. Respect the confusion or emptiness. Often, there is fear of healing as it presents the unknown. Sometimes, after you've poured in all the positive energy, when the negativity and grief leave, there is emptiness. It can be frightening to feel the void. Accept this, and embrace the new. Trust that answers will come; have faith that the right people and situations will present themselves. This is a tough one if you have not previously believed this way.

Living with a sense of order is another form of self care. Structure also encourages us to be strong. Abe Frischer was the patriarch of a family close to mine. We have celebrated holidays together for the last nineteen years. When Abe passed away I was particularly touched by what I learned about him at his funeral. His grandson told of how Abe lived by his values, sense of honor and responsibility. He had become a success in business, more than once. Like many, he had gone through challenging periods. At one point, his office was in his house. He would wake up every morning at five, don his suit and tie then go to the room in his house that had become his office. Such discipline. He taught by example that structure in life allows for strength, even when we don't *feel* strong. He was a man who had faced many obstacles with a positive attitude, a personal code of ethics, discipline and warmth of spirit. He did not let events dictate how he ran his life; rather, his backbone provided the framework, no matter what happened.

The esteemed psychologist, Abraham Maslow, puts self actualization at the top of the developmental pyramid. We are never at that point as we are always growing (or stagnating) until the end; but we can always be in a state of "actualizing". Even when we feel we are regressing, we may actually be preparing to go further forward. An excellent visualization to call upon is of Diana, the goddess of the Moon and the Hunt. When preparing for battle, she would pull the bow back as far as she could. It would sometimes appear as if she were stuck in a backwards stance but then she would release the bow and it would it shoot further forward than ever before.

What are you preparing for? It doesn't matter where you are in your development, just that when you find, or create your place, claim it and move in.

This is where vision comes into play. When you create a vision for a new pattern, you must give it a life force more vital than the old one. You need to convince yourself that it is real. Use your senses and emotions to bring it to life: what does it look, smell or feel like? The more you visualize (and experience) the new pattern, the more real and compelling it becomes. See the person you want to be and then become her.

EXERCISE:

Inhale and imagine flying in the sky through the whitest, most billowy clouds. Exhale as you allow yourself to drift. Let your mind rest on the cottony surface. You are in bliss. Step softly, looking for just the right spot to lie down. Feel the clouds surrounding and caressing you. Be aware of floating and of being alone. You are comfortable, at peace.

Inhale. Let the greatest challenge you are now facing come to the forefront of your consciousness. Take a moment and review how you have been handling the situation. Exhale. Acknowledge how well you have done and explore other possible options. Perhaps choose one new action, thought or belief that could also work towards the solution.

The question; *how old are you in this conversation*, is a marker along the road, a guidepost for checking your progress. The child in us is always present and may cooperate, or resist depending on our emotional age. How mature is your approach? Do you hear your nurturing voice telling you how to get through this? What is it saying?

Breathe.

Now listen to your voice of reason, the voice of structure. What is it suggesting? What practical advice for dealing with a particular challenge is the voice advising?

While breathing, check for any thoughts, beliefs or feelings that weigh you down. Be aware of nostalgia, sadness, grief, resentments or judgment. Breathe and release these into the clouds. All toxins and negativity will transform into clean air.

Be aware of how empty and light you now feel. Notice if you are supported and safe.

Slowly open your eyes (without coming down off the cloud) and write what you see, feel and think about what you have just experienced.

Know that you can return to this spot whenever you desire. You can create a vision of freedom and space in previously tight mental, emotional, and physical places. This is a trustworthy prescription for freedom and expansive vision that lies at the heart of transforming your life.

What fresh patterns are you now willing to see and adopt?

Meredith came to class one day after doing the previous exercise. She recalled being stuck in an overwhelming, new job. Her husband had left her with three young children and, of course, no money. She had taken a job that she hated but it had the promise of prosperity. She was filled with anxiety and fear each morning.

One day she telephoned her closest friend while at her desk. As she moaned her plight into the phone, her friend Ilene asked, "Did you bring lunch with you today?" "Yes," Meredith answered, "but what does that have to do with anything?' "Did you bring it in a brown paper bag?" "Yes," Meredith answered, exasperated, but trusting that her friend was going to help. "Well," said Ilene, "Take the bag into the ladies' room and go into a stall. Empty the bag and hold the top while you breathe into it. You are hyperventilating. You are allowing events outside yourself to take control. You need to get oxygen back into your lungs. You are just experiencing fear. After you do this put the lunch back in the bag, comb your hair, put fresh lipstick on and get back to work!"

Meredith, who later became a very successful real estate agent, shared that she had forgotten how young she had been emotionally at the time of the crisis. She had forgotten about her panic, that first job and how funny it all seemed in retrospect. She told us that she will once again use the anchor of the brown bag rescue when she needs to reclaim her sanity, calm down and remind herself that she is safe.

When starting a new pattern, or during times of stress, the lure of old patterns is strong. Practice helps make the new programming more powerful than the old; the more we reinforce new commands, the stronger they become.

If we bask in the light of positive energy we will see healthy patterns begin to emerge and the old, dysfunctional murkiness will fade away. We often stop writing all together when faced with hard decisions. You can easily forget all the positive re-enforcement and revert to old, comforting ways. Understanding what can trigger a relapse and rededicating yourself to the practice prevents backsliding further. This is a good time to ask:

How can my practice be more reflective?

____

____

What do I need to work on?

____

____

What sends me into a tailspin?

____

Each element builds on the previous one. Together these become instruments for change.

When you articulate your worst fears they dissolve.

Stephanie was dealing with breast cancer when her husband had a heart attack. Although he survived, she experienced panic attacks every morning which didn't subside until lunchtime. I suggested that she ask herself in writing what she was afraid of. She actually had a written dialogue with the panic and let it tell her what she needed to do. Relaxation exercises combined with the writing brought her almost instant and long-lasting relief. "I'm not taking any chances. I do not want to see the return of any panic. I roll out of bed, do some breathing and visualizing and then write for about ten minutes, even before I brush my teeth or greet my husband. This is my idea of extreme self care. I'm a believer!"

EXERCISE:

You are in a circular room. It is surrounded by windows. You cannot see outside because the light turns the view to crystal. The space you are in is breathtakingly beautiful. You stand in the center on an illuminated floor.

You may feel slightly off balance but know that you are gently supported from behind although no one else is with you.

Float down to the floor and sit, cross-legged, shoulders relaxed and straight, posture beautiful. Breathe in.

As you rest ask: who are the people, places and things I care most about, the ones who are crucial to my well-being?

____

____

____

____

____

Listen to what they are saying about caring for yourself.

Listen closely to your own heart. What messages are coming through?

____

____

Leave this magical room, knowing that you can return here as often as you'd like. Record what you've just experienced.

KNITTING

When I think of knots within me
I see balls of wool appearing
With miles of clear long strands
Resistance comes to mind
And how to break the pattern
That has matured with passing time

Dissolving seems an answer
Just a little here and there
Like melting piles of ice
That are forming everywhere

As the icicles transform
Into rivers or to streams
They flow on down the mountain
And melt into my dreams

And then suddenly a knot
Has formed within my hands

Did I take my attention off it
Losing sight of the moving ball
The moment disappearing
As I slip into recall

Just bring my focus back
To the here and now I saw
So the knitting can transport me
To the seamless art of play

Ruth Netter

Exercise:

With closed eyes, think of creating more room so that the knots of stress can disappear. Breathe. See what thoughts come.

Create space physically, emotionally, and mentally.

Breathe. Think about your ability to receive from others. In your mind's eye weigh your "receiving hand" with your "giving hand". Are they balanced? Although we have all heard that it is better to give than to receive, it is only half true. Drift to the place where you feel deserving.

Your purpose is to love, to both give and receive it. I also believe that wishes, dreams and desires are the messages about who you are and what you want to accomplish. I've never had the desire to sing opera (good thing, seeing as I'm tone deaf) but I've always wanted to write; but allowing family dysfunctions to override my *wise woman voice* prevented me from moving forward.

What wise woman? When we were children we did not possess all our wisdom. Often it was knocked out of us or a curtain was drawn across it. We were not in our power. Now we are, or at least on the way. Go with what feels right. Have compassion for the little girl you once were but be here now, in the present as a woman.

FLOW

Be,
As water is,
Without friction.

Flow around the edges
Of those within your path.
Surround within your ever-moving depths
Those who come to rest there
Enfold them,
While never for a moment holding on.

Accept whatever distance
Others are moved within your flow.
Be with them gently
As far as they allow your strength to take them,
And fill with your own being
The remaining space when they are left behind.

When dropping down life's rapids,
Froth and bubble into fragments if you must,
Knowing that the one of you now many
Will just as many times be one again.

And when you've gone as far as you can go,
Quietly await your next beginning.

Anonymous

Extreme self care time is a period of recovery. Honor what you have unearthed and processed, allowing for a transition back into the present. Release the steam of old hurts, betrayals and loss gently with love and compassion for all you have endured. It is time now (if not now, when?) to step into your brilliance and become free.

AFFIRMATION:

I am strong and have compassion towards myself and others.

SUMMARY:

- Extreme self care, which includes writing, is mandatory!
- The support of others can be a beacon when the way is lost.
- It takes time to learn new patterns of thought and behavior.
- To create a new vision, a life force more vital than the previous one is needed.
- Bask in the light of positive energy and healthy patterns begin to emerge as the old, dysfunctional murkiness fades away.

CHAPTER SIX:

ARRIVE AND BE PRESENT

Caretaker of Contentment

The state beyond success is artistry
— Anonymous

Once upon a time in Japan, an old man found a cocoon in his garden. He watched and waited for it to open, for the butterfly to emerge. Days went by as he saw it straining from within. In an effort to help the creature birth itself, he gently picked the cocoon up and opened it. The butterfly started to take flight and then fell to the ground and died. Nature commands that we struggle out of our individual wombs as we are born through life's first challenge.

Writing, and other means of expression, teach patience and the art of surrendering control of that which cannot be changed. With strength and courage you have committed to healing a lifetime of accumulated wounds. Now it is time to celebrate, to rejoice in having arrived at contentment, a place of pride for who you have become. Be aware of the possibilities and accepting that which cannot be changed; be conscious that it is a choice to be positive and content, no matter what is going on all around or within. All this and more has been accomplished. It may put you into the category of heroine, humanitarian or just a wise, peaceful woman, a woman of strength and beauty.

EXERCISE:

Allow yourself to come to your private, open space.

Breathe in and become aware of your surroundings. Breathe out. As you inhale imagine being wrapped up snugly in yards and yards of silken cloth. Exhale.

Feel safe and nurtured. Inhale.

Exhale.

Inhale and think of an area in your life where there may be something minor you still would like to relieve. Exhale. Inhale breathing in clean, pure air while cleansing whatever wound or toxin that remains.

Notice if there is a habit of repeated thought that continues to prevent you from being in your highest self. It is when we are aware of a repeated pattern, and commit to change, that we can truly fly, free of past controls.
As you exhale, gently release the problem. You have the ability to let it go by caring for yourself above all else. Remember that you are safe in the present moment.

As you exhale, gently release the problem. You have the ability to let it go by caring for yourself above all else. Remember that you are safe in the present moment.

Affirmation:

Have the intention to dwell in your soul, listening to its whispering each day, and knowing that it will bring you to the heart of any situation.

Remember that you love and are loved unconditionally; writing and healthy self-talk guide as you are given what is needed and wanted. Your radiance will manifest brighter than ever. Although this work won't grant you a reprieve from a terminal illness or bring the return of a departed loved one, it will teach acceptance, gratitude and patience. Debbie Ford writes, "Ask for what your soul needs and your heart desires." Let us be human in our imperfection and at peace with ourselves. Above all, let's practice gratitude for what is, not remorse for what is not.

Gratitude Journals have proven to be very successful. People regularly list things they appreciate; some spend a few moments every evening reviewing their day and finding at least five good things to acknowledge. Others start their day with a list, anecdote or dream which shifts the focus to blessings instead of flaws or struggles. Over time, the mind shifts into a positive state without conscious thought. We didn't become negative in a day so it takes quite a while to achieve lasting change. Let us be patient, focused and determined.

You have learned how to separate feelings from thoughts, knowing that most fear, terror and anxiety are feelings from the past or about the future. You are safe in the moment. Remember to reframe any situation and ask: **Where am I in time?** Training to ask this question teaches assimilation of what is to come without reacting with worry.

Confronting a concern that reoccurred after being free of it for twenty years, Tina wrote, *In the last few days my life seems to have ground to a halt. I know that's bogus, but that's how I feel. Now that I'm learning not to ruminate about the past or project into the future, I am still. I have felt like a victim most of my life. Now I can take responsibility and am ready to move on. I want to get started but find myself still sitting here, getting in touch with gratitude for the first time in my life. I am so filled with awareness as I write this. I know how rare it is to have this very precious time and space before I go into the fray again. Now I am so very grateful for the way my life is unfolding.*

Remember that if you have grown up with negativity, criticism and complaint, the thought that nothing is ever good enough produces more of the same. In order to enjoy life we must learn to appreciate what we do have instead of bemoaning what we don't. Abundance is a state of mind.

If we allow it, writing will reveal addictions. My mother was a Monday morning quarter-back her whole life. She could even rehash and reanalyze conversations and situations from thirty years ago. I was aware of how dysfunctional this was and tried to gently point it out when I saw that it caused her to re-experience painful feelings. I thought that there was no point to it. Through my writing, I came to see that I had unconsciously picked up the same habit. I got to write about the feelings this addiction produced. It was a sickeningly sweet state of suspension, a numb place that brought me immediately back to being stuck. I thought I was doing it to learn from my mistakes. I realized that I had never really improved or changed; I was stuck in an endless groove of a scratched CD. It hasn't been easy to undo the programming but it becomes easier, and faster, each time I become conscious that I am doing it.

We talk about all sorts of things in writing class as life experiences provide fertile ground for writing. This week we spoke of dogs.

Sarah received a much-wanted puppy this summer. Clive is a Labradoodle, a picture perfect pup, except he is irascible. In class Sarah told how she had finally broken down and watched a dog-training show. The host was advising his guest to tell herself that she was Cleopatra and her dog was just her dog, not a person. The dog was to walk beside or behind her, never in front; she was the queen.

It dawned on me that our minds are like puppies that need to be trained. Left to their own devices our brains often run into the street. Minds are meant to be unsatisfied, to solve problems, to try to control. We must take them by the hand or lead them by a leash, keeping our hearts and our souls open, not controlled. Our souls are the empresses, the true monarchs.

Our minds will stop us from healing in order to keep our scripts alive. The stories of our lives that we keep telling ourselves seem real. Were we really the victim of whatever has befallen us? What are the benefits of being a victim? We get attention, are nurtured (or not), get rescued (or not). What happens when we're self-reliant? Our minds don't know what to do with that too easily. We must be strong if we're to be self-reliant; we have to take responsibility for our own needs and happiness. If we trust ourselves and remain impartial, we will not set ourselves up for disappointment. If we strive to stay in a place of unconditional love, then we can remain happy although others may behave in manipulative ways.

EXERCISE:

Close your eyes and rest, becoming attuned to the rhythm of the breath. Breathe in and focus on how this simple act which occurs without prompting sustains you. How miraculous.

Release, inhale and think of the shade of blue in the sky which pleases you most. Be thankful that you are here to experience such things. Exhale.

Now think of something that brings you joy. Let the thought fill your whole being. As you exhale release any pain you are conscious of experiencing. Inhale. Think of someone you love. Feel the experience of a hug from that individual; as you exhale, release a frustration or annoyance you may have with someone else. Just let it go.

Ask yourself to name a hundred things for which you are grateful. Think of hearing a baby's cooing, smelling something fabulous cooking on someone's stove or feeling fine silk or velvet. Taste a favored wine or some delicacy you adore. Take your time. When you have gotten as far as you can, slowly open your eyes and record as many items as you can remember, then write about how you feel.

As adults we are responsible for our own happiness. In illness or death we can elect to choose contentment over resentment, to live and die with dignity, strength and grace. As the Dalai Lama states, "happiness is an art".

Here it all is. At this point in the book all tools have been set out, sharpened and polished.

Many of us have been told that we are too chaotic or messy, tightly wound or anal. Some need order to see and think clearly, others need to abandon strong structure. There is no one correct way; find *the balance* that suits you. You will know when you have reached it because you will feel peace and contentment. Just as chaos has its own order, according to the philosopher Nietzsche, so does your particular course.

EXERCISE:

Inhale and imagine walking down a country road. This could be somewhere you've actually been, or a place you are now creating.

Exhale.

Breathe in the natural fragrances. Exhale and see an attractive sign by the side of the road. The lettering reads CONTENTMENT with an arrow pointing to a path. Curious, you walk up this trail, intuitively knowing that this is where you belong. You view the garden and mansion, or maybe you find a cottage. As you stroll, notice that not all is perfect. There are some repairs to be done. As you stroll to the edge of a lake, notice a boat and a box. This box contains tools that you will use throughout life.

Carefully examine the exterior of the box. Is it made of old wood, metal, ebony, mahogany, silver or gold? Is it encrusted with jewels, shells, or stones? Perhaps it's made of cake or feathers. Let your imagination play. Perhaps it is a carrying case made entirely of flowers which will never wilt.

Sit by the side of the lake as you peruse the contents of the box. What tools will you need to maintain the balance between what needs to be repaired, what you are unable to fix, and what needs to be accepted as is?

When you are ready, allow yourself to come gently back into the room and begin to write about what was revealed to you and what you visualized. Write about what tools you need to live in contentment with everything fine tuned and in its best shape.

Know that your individual toolbox is available to you at all times and contains all you will ever need. Some find it helpful to check on their tools every morning, even before they get out of bed.

We are like drops of rain falling into the river. We *can* go with the flow and travel gently whichever way the current takes us. This is contentment.

How many of us remember the expression "Go with the flow"? It became very popular in the 60's when most of us wanted the world to 'chill' and we didn't trust anyone over thirty. Naïve? Perhaps just a bit. Who could have imagined what it would take to acquire wisdom which is usually attained through life experience?

Allow yourself to visualize a decision you must now make which is causing frustration. Can you imagine yourself flowing with whichever way you choose to go? You may want to write about it.

CONTENTMENT

I think contentment is a form of acceptance combined with gratitude. Enjoyment enters into it. There are various forms that come at different times in one's life

When I was young, I loved playing with my friends, unhindered by adult supervision. We acted out our fantasies in the form of made-up plays to which we charged admission. Our curtain was an old sheet hung across the garage and the audience was composed mostly of doting grandmothers.

As a teenager, contentment was sipping a thick milkshake at the local spa, preferably with a boyfriend.

As a bride and later a mother, contentment changed. It consisted of silence instead of chaos when everything seemed to be in place, the children were well and happy and all appliances worked!

But through the years, there runs a thread. I am always content when lost in a good book. From early days in my grandfather's house, when I was a drummer boy who died with Napoleon's *army, to teenage years on rainy days in the* Catskills, *when I lived far away in time and place, as* Catherine of Aragon, *to my old age when I am at leisure to peruse* P.D. James, Marilynne Robinson, *and the latest "best-sellers", I am content.*

AJ Malloy

LIMITATIONS

Many limitations are self imposed. Some are not. Can you visualize drifting past all of them, being energized by all the extra electricity contentment provides? Perhaps you can visualize a tunnel which goes under and through any limitation you now face. Have fun with this. Allow yourself to unfurl wings and fly over the limits you have named.

Write. Write and let you inner voice take you where you need to go. Keep letting go. After you have written ask yourself how you feel. If you don't feel uplifted write again. Go further, higher and with more breadth that you ever have before.

Notice if there is a habit of repeated thought that continues to prevent you from being in your highest self. It is when we are aware of a repeated pattern, and commit to change, that we can truly fly, free of past controls.

As J. M. Barrie wrote in **Peter Pan**, "This has happened before and it will happen again." Let us learn from the past and from others who have paved the way. We no longer have to repeat undesirable patterns.

Be willing to bring your struggle to the light and let the radiance bring about contentment. Feel yourself supported by love.

CONFLICT

We all know by now that conflict is a part of life. We are problem solving beings. Sometimes not making a choice is even a solution.

Know that conflict is neither good nor bad, positive nor negative it just is. Imagine cooperating with conflicts, the interferences in life. Watch them transform into resolutions. As we write about our dilemmas, the atoms of conflict change structure and so do we. If we release our beliefs or just loosen them a bit, all answers will come.

Whatever challenge or difficulty you are confronting know that your commitment will bring peace. As in martial arts or dance, if you step back the opponent steps forward. Remove yourself from the contest and accept what exists. This leads to peace.

Life cannot necessarily be understood; life can be accepted or rejected. If we accept what 'is' we are, in a sense, rejuvenated. We live moments of transformative awareness. Writing insures heightened awareness. Great writing communicates this sensitivity to others and is called art. Our stories as well as our lives have profound meaning. They remind us that we matter and that we have fulfilled our obligation to express our selves, no matter how confusing or painful it may be.

Through our writing we realize that what befalls us doesn't define us; courage, tenacity and a way of being in the world does.

Rebecca, a young widow told the class, *"I keep writing because it allows me to leave all the loss, the grief, and angst at the door so I can be with myself again."* If you don't handle an issue (such as procrastination, laziness, lack of self worth) and you think that you've escaped it this time you are deluding yourself. It will crop up again and again throughout your life until it is handled. Each time it comes back it is stronger, louder, more challenging to address. Anna Freud, Sigmund's daughter and also a psychologist, said that in the beginning the universe gives us wide berth to knock around and make mistakes. As we grow older the corridors close in, our chances narrow and life becomes more intense. I love that.

How do you know when you're content? Close your eyes for a moment and think of all the things this word means to you. When you're ready, open your eyes and allow yourself to write about who the caretaker of your contentment is and what it means to you.

Contentment is lying in bed next to Larry while he is sleeping knowing that my kids are warm and placidly sleeping in their beds too. As the sun peeks through the darkness of the tree tops surrounding our windows I lie there waiting to fall back into slumber as this is one of those rare occasions that I do not have to rise with the sun. Ahh, my house is full of the people I love and we are all together', I think as I drift off.

The caretaker of my contentment has to be me. I love that phrase: caretaker of my contentment. It invites and promises. It makes me think of gardening, something I love to do. The phrase makes it seem possible to actually grow contentment. Watch it start as a small sigh, a seed, then the twinkle of a yellow flower that will fruit at the end of a leafy stalk, growing slowly as it changes from green to red and becomes a plump, heavy tomato pulling the vine towards the ground and releasing.

Contentment is perhaps not something you grow, but maybe something you cultivate. And it requires vigilance, the constant weeding out of negative thoughts. You can't get annoyed at the weeds, they always come-just as negative thoughts do. But rather than spend a lot of time pulling weeds, I have learned to mulch. You can keep weeds from growing by keeping them from the sun, in the darkness under the mulch. No sun, no weeds, oh occasionally a few but so few the effort to pull them out is minimal, mindless, like shooing away a fly. So, how do you mulch negative thoughts? Keep pouring in the clear water I guess. Pull yourself out from the darkness, stand in the sunshine with your eyes closed and imagine the rays going through you, into you, lighting you up, filling you with radiance.

Recently, while in yoga class, for the first time ever, I could see my body, my skin like a tunnel, my arms themselves like sleeves. I saw the darkness inside my body as a place where a light could shine and I momentarily understood that I could be its conduit.

Contentment itself is the sunshine that radiates warmth and light. Contentment is that happy emotion that sits quietly and doesn't need to jump up and down for joy. If you sit still long enough contentment can calmly infuse your soul, like tea leaves in hot water.

The seed of contentment, I believe, is gratitude. Within a minute of starting to think of what you are grateful for, the first things being children, partner, home, garden, food, music, you realize you can just keeping going forever, apple pie, socks still warm from the dryer, pens scratching against paper, on and on.

Contentment is actually a wonderful goal as well as a state of mind: it is a bright yellow ribbon rolling off its spool. Contentment is uncluttered, and finally I am uncluttering now that I am almost done with the construction of the house. Uncluttering feels so good and has been happening. Like a fever, I am beset by fall cleaning, why is it the colder air and the falling leaves bring on the impulse?

Contentment doesn't allow for overages, doesn't like too much, doesn't need 'wow already', because it is firmly rooted in the now.

The caretaker of my contentment is me. I can create it for myself and while I may not be able to create it for others at least I can sprinkle it liberally around, like seeds broadcast upon the ground.

I think I would like to write a paragraph with some of the phrases from today's discussions and put them by my mirror and say them over and over every morning. Perhaps the same is true for the change I want to make that I was speaking of earlier. Ten new sentences every morning to start the day, over and over. Then if, or better to say when, it works a different set for next year. With less to grumble to myself about myself the more continuous my contentment, the less cautious my contentment, the more concrete and real it becomes. I guess it's possible, even a rock can grow fatter if it rolls through concrete.

Loretta Cummings

Loretta wrote all of the above in her gratitude journal while dealing with a chronic disease. She found that the writing soothed and stretched her, all the way back to health.

Of course, tools, mantras and reminders such as affirmations create the space to be content even in the worst of circumstances. It is the mind that confounds, confuses and constricts. Hearts and souls know what is real and true.

So, here is a refresher on where to go and what to do when things get rough. If you've practiced enough you can just go into your breath. The old adage about counting to ten actually works especially if the breaths are deep and rhythmic. For those times when you need a bit more try this:

Exercise:

Allow your eyes to gently close.

Feel yourself float up towards one of those soft billowy clouds. Inhale. Feel your body cocooned within the cloud and relax.

Glance down to the earth below. See those you love, those with whom you interact and sometimes have issues. You realize that you can be with them but not attached to the 'stuff' of any interaction. You are a part of all you love, not dependent or triggered by anyone or anything. Breathe. Glance down and ask yourself what is real. Breathe. If you can feel yourself lovingly detaching, do so now. Breathe and remember that you have the ability to return to this place, with open eyes, whenever you desire.

Receptivity

One of the best ways to learn extreme self care is to become conscious of how you behave around the area of receiving. Many of us are nurturers and we often forget about caring for ourselves. We speak of being "givers" or "takers" as if these were our basic, unchangeable natures. Monitor your thoughts and actions; learn how to create, or keep, the balance. Observe your pattern of giving in ratio to what you allow yourself to receive.

When I give, I feel...

____

____

____.

When I take or allow myself to receive, I feel...

____

____

____.

If you unearth some unsettling emotions you might want to write on this topic extensively. This is a wonderful way to transform some deep seated beliefs about worthiness. Be sure to ask how much you give to yourself and how much you take away.

A number of years ago I considered quitting a job where my position had changed, drastically. The particular qualities which brought me joy and fulfillment had been eliminated and the bureaucracy had taken over. I was lost in confusion as to what the message was for me. I was rattled with doubt about leaving the job's security. I knew I could look at the situation as an opportunity. I had pipe dreams of what I would then do, but I was fearful of taking the plunge.

I decided to attend a weekend conference given by Omega Institute, the center for holistic studies. Fortuitously, there happened to be the second annual weekend conference, called Living Fearlessly, scheduled for later that month. Many wise and famous speakers spoke; as I attended various workshops I was receptive to finding my answers, although doubted that they would come in the way that they did.

During the first break I got on the very long line to the ladies' room. Nothing unusual but I was irritated that the entire time until the next workshop would be taken up with standing on line with the other thirty or so women. 'We are in a hotel in Manhattan,' I thought, as I left the line, noticing how it was growing. I took the stairs to the next floor and went through the door that said Executive Suites. It was Saturday and only the cleaning lady was working on that floor. She assured me it would be fine to use the luxurious facilities. As I returned to the conference wing and noticed some of the same women still on line the thought hit me; I AM RESOURCEFUL! When I wrote, the realization that while I may be scatter-brained, disorganized and a lot of other things which impede my progress, I always find a solution that works for me. I will be fine, leaving this job; I will find my way, I will be successful; those thoughts all came tumbling out of a place within me that I couldn't access through weeks of pro and con lists, talking with friends or communing with nature. Only writing allows me to dial up and listen to my intuition.

If we believe our negative, unhealthy thoughts we suffer. These thoughts create the downward spiral of rage, depression, sorrow and helplessness.

If we choose not to believe these limiting and excruciating, often unconscious, thoughts we can be healthy.

Writing is the sword to cut through the dragon of discontent. It can reveal our true essence and the sheer joy we experienced as infants when just our basic needs were met.

Through writing we can investigate which beliefs inspire us and which ones limit or sabotage. We can discover the truth of our beliefs and the possibility of changing them. We can examine who we want to be and start the practice of being that person, now.

Through writing we can expose the qualities we possess which allow us to thrive. Often they are attributes that we see in others and they may see in us but we are unaware of in ourselves.

Writing keeps probing us, asking what we really want to say. Most of all, writing reignites curiosity and passion. It asks us to pay attention to life-its pain and joy, the hot and cold. It asks who we were earlier in our lives and when on the path we went to sleep, woke up, made love and learned how to fill our very souls. It reminds us who we are and what others mean to us. It lays bare our emotional truth in the search for meaning, and that, dear reader is healing.

This is *your* write to heal; tell it to yourself, your loved ones or the world; it's a great story!

Let us be human in our imperfection and at peace with ourselves. Above all, let's practice gratitude for what is, not discontent for what isn't.

> *As I was growing up I discovered writing as a way to get in touch with my deepest feelings. Somehow the written word seemed more profound than the spoken one and exposed thoughts and emotions I would not have found other-wise. On*

paper my words would stare at me. After my son's death, I took pen to hand and began a journey. Words glared, cried, smiled and provoked; they were mine to ponder, change, analyze or rearrange. I would question and come to know their true identity.

I traveled into the darkness of my inner universe searching for meaning and enlightenment. I tried to catch the outer spirit with the inner soul. I threw my vision to the heavens asking for guidance and help in finding the meaning to life while I felt lost and helpless. Through observation, reading, meditation and writing, I came to understand and accept nature's way. I still stumble and get caught in traps, but I have learned how to release my soul and right my spirit.

May each see deep inside to understand that every moment is new, as the past becomes a memory of experience and the future a continuing journey.

If we can accept life as a constant changing wind, perhaps we can ride on it, not in turmoil but with peace.

Pat Rosenberg

AFFIRMATION:

I deserve what I desire. I am willing to have faith. My soul continues to manifest. I am vigilant to the positive nature of my thoughts. My thoughts lead to positive feelings. I am always willing to adjust and grow.

I was named Lynda for my grandmother, Leah. She died, a victim of dysfunction, while my mother was pregnant with me. Her voice was never heard, her story never told. I have adopted Leah's name in honor of her and all the other women who struggle to be heard, who need to tell their tales, so that we all can continue to heal. We all have that write.

In light and love,
Leah

ADDITIONAL EXERCISES

I

Most people have experienced angst-driven times during adolescence. Challenging though they may be, these are usually experiences where growth takes place. The Pulitzer Prize winning author Michael Chabon claims that it was because of this time locked in his attic that he began to write, and has continued to do so. He wrote because it unleashed his imagination at a time when real life seemed bleak. He was constantly nourished by the imagination of others and wished to do the same for somebody else, somewhere trapped in his or her own loneliness.

Rest in your usual spot, or choose someplace new. Close your eyes and let your memory take you back to your teenage years. As if looking through a photo album from that time, drift along capturing images of when you listened to certain music while feeling miserable, when you read particular books to counteract the loneliness or perhaps watched a movie when in despair.

See the names of the movies, music or literature that kept you company at that time. Now, as if spinning a game wheel, watch where the spinner stops and chooses one of the memories. Write about how and why this memory helped form you. Was it a catalyst in unleashing your imagination and is there some wisdom you can now pass along to others? Really take yourself back to that time, whether it was generally pleasant or not. Perhaps the emotional state was just a quick episode or maybe it was a pervasive state-of-being.

Allow yourself creative freedom with this; recreate the clothes you wore, your bedroom, the foods you ate and the friends you kept. You survived the time and matured. Many who do this exercise unearth new insight into who they were and how differently they are able to handle things now. Some find the source of their oversensitivity or weakness. They often make present-day changes with the newfound awareness that materializes through the pen.

"The world breaks everyone and afterward many are strong at the broken places."

— Ernest Hemingway

II

Repair: At some point in your life you must have needed to fix something. Maybe you hadn't wanted to; you may have thought that you were unskilled or incapable. Did you ever get stuck by the side of the road with a flat tire and no one else was around, did you ever want to wear a brooch or necklace that was broken? Did a child's toy need immediate attention or a bargain in a store beckon, even though you needed to fix it in order to use it?

Close your eyes and drift back in your memory bank to just one incident. Take the first memory that pops up. Remember that the unconscious can access these memories in unfathomable ways; all you need to do is be quiet and let your inner voice speak.

Recall this incident where you rose to the occasion and fixed what was needed. Describe where you were and what the circumstances were. Describe your thoughts and feelings at the time, especially how you felt when you completed your task. If you are able to, draw a parallel to what you are experiencing in your life at the present time. Identify the qualities that moved you to action then and see if you can locate them now; can you apply the same resourcefulness now, even though the particulars are different? Recall the feelings of completion and success.

III

Gently breathe in through your nose. Breathe out, softly. Close your eyes. Now breathe in forcefully, just beyond your comfort zone. Exhale as if trying to blow out a fire which is about to blaze out of control. Pause and note whatever feelings arise. Is there a sense of discomfort or fear, of losing ground, of hyperventilating? Let go…notice that you are really safe.

Identify what the fear feels like. Think of one or two frightening examples from your real life. Did you fail to take a promotion because it felt unsafe? Were you afraid to speak out in a group or dive off a high board over a lake? Did you shy away from doing things you wanted to do in your life because of fear?

Now imagine hiding in a cave, surrounded by darkness. Suddenly the surface opens up and reveals the evening sky, the moon resting on a bed of clouds.

All you need to do is float as you release, release and release the fear. Feel yourself relaxing. Know that you have always done your best with whatever information was available.

Come back to the room and write about a period of your life when you didn't 'go for it'. Write with compassion for who you were. If you had known better you would have made different choices. Now you can recognize and comfort that part of you which couldn't trust. Explore the reasons and write about how you've grown. If you are still cynical or skeptical, discuss that on the page. The only rule is that you do it without judgment and that you are honest. Perhaps the opportunities aren't the same but dreams and goals are always within reach. Remember; goals are dreams with deadlines.

Whatever is held on to, whatever is undigested turns rancid. For years I carried tremendous regret for a lost opportunity. My husband and I had been living in England, learning how to run my in-laws' historic fifty bedroom hotel and restaurant so they could retire. When I realized that they would never leave and we would be living under their roof for thirty or forty years, I begged to go back to America. For years after we returned I was haunted by the disappointment over having given up a most interesting life. It wasn't until I started writing about it that I was able to release all the negative emotions associated with running away. Through describing how I had just given birth in a foreign country without friends and family around and with my husband being forced to work eighteen hours a day, I was able to develop compassion for the young, lonely woman I had been. Through seeing the story on the page I was able to get in touch with my in-laws' critical and tyrannical ways; most of all I developed pride in how I nurtured my new-born baby girl (without any healthy role-models) and stood up to what in reality was too drastic a price for what was being offered. I finally came to a place where I accepted the fact that I had been ruled by fear and found peace in the realization that I had even tried. I also developed compassion for my in-laws and was able to make my peace with them.

Allow yourself to sit now with your feet on the ground, hands uncrossed.
Breathe in through your nose. Imagine your breath traveling up and through your head as it clears and swirls away any recognizable cobwebs from the past.

Now survey your body and release toxins such as shame, unwarranted embarrassment, hopelessness, resentment, jealousy or anger anywhere you notice that they reside. Take as long as you like. When you are ready slowly open your eyes and write about your awareness of a toxicity that you have been harboring for a long, long time. Begin to write. You may find that you are having a conversation with a substantive emotion. Some even call the negative voice an entity. Some hear a parent's voice; the nun, doctor, teacher or anyone who has turned their thoughts in this direction can come through in the writing. Allow the voice to surface without attachment. See when and where you began to listen. Now that you know better you are able to let it all go.

IV

Open your breathing to its largest capacity. Observe what happens when you do this. Stay in neutral-watch as if you are at the back of a train; leave the stress at the station.

With eyes closed, ask yourself to name the five people who upset you most in your life. As you review each one step back and comment, 'Isn't that interesting?'

Now imagine if you had responded to the people who upset you in this way. Perhaps you couldn't have said these words out loud but meditating on the expression will keep you in neutral, what the Buddhists call Being the Witness. Come back into the room and write about one of the noted upsets. Choose to either write a new ending to the story or just observe what would have changed if you had maintained a neutral state.

V

No one can measure the loss of a loved one. But there are other losses endured which can be reframed; the losses can add up and diminish you, if permitted to whittle away your joy. Losing a friendship, a favorite picture or letter can be debilitating to any degree allowed. Consider such a loss as the throwing off of old clothing which is no longer in good condition. Perhaps what you have lost no longer fits who you have become. Ask the change what it is telling you. When you close your eyes and breathe rhythmically and softly for a few minutes can you see how you have learned, grown or benefitted from your loss? Come back to the room and write about it.

VI

Question what you believe: when you question your thoughts, what you believe is often in need of an update. After meditating for a three minute period ask yourself if there is a belief that you hold that is causing you pain. Do not go unconscious; rather be in a state of observation. What is a relationship or situation that is now causing you to be upset, frustrated or angry?

Examine the beliefs you have in regards to an outcome and ask if you can change the belief in order to obtain a desired result. For instance, if you are angry with your sister because she is critical and you are often hurt by her comments, ask if you can see the situation as one that has little to do with you. Is she generally intolerant with everyone? Does she lack manners in her dealing with just you? Can you believe that it is her lack and indeed has nothing to do with your not being worthy? Play with the scenario in writing and see what happens. Write a different outcome.

VII

"Arrange whatever pieces come your way" **—Virginia Woolf**

Although Woolf suffered from mental illness before she took her own life she wrote profoundly about human character showing extraordinary insight into the human psyche and soul. What do you think that she meant by arranging pieces that come your way? How can this be a tool, a coping mechanism? Write about the above statement and what your suffering has produced. What deep knowledge have you acquired in your lifetime from such trials and tribulations?

VIII

"We all hide in the open secret" **—Rumi**

So much suffering stems from feeling separate, alien from the rest of life, lacking in connection. Notice the increase in depression and desperation that is reported around the holidays. How much suffering in your life has involved feeling as if you are the only one to have gone through loss and difficulty?

Close your eyes now and know that you are not really alone, nor have you ever been-it may have just felt that way. When you reached out wasn't an individual or some power always there? Breathe in the reality that we are all connected on some deep, profound level. Interpret the statement Rumi wrote in the twelfth century. In writing, ask and answer what ways you hide out in the open, probably in ways that others see. Is it possible that with the revealed information you might be able to choose to see differently? Explore the possibilities.

IX

How do you maintain the connection deep within yourself without losing awareness of the world outside? You slow down. Close your eyes now and take a deep breath. Slow down now by sitting for a while with your breath. Check the pace of your recent past. Have you been annoyed more than usual? Are you feeling more anger and stress than you know is healthy? Are you eating more, or less than is normal for you? Are you tired most of the time?

Now imagine a perfect day, one where you stay connected to your rich inner life. How do you awaken? Where are you? What do you do in the first hour of the day? What practices or rituals do you allow yourself? What do you eat, wear and do?

Now imagine a point in the day where you may falter, such as a 4:00 slump. Is it when you lose the thread of connection? Have the courage and faith to wait in stillness until you find it again. Describe how you do that. Do you give yourself a cup of herb tea, a warm bath, a phone call or walk with a friend? Slowly come back into the room and take up your pen. Write about living that day.

Or, write about a day, or days, when you flit about without awareness and devise a plan to now focus. List what small steps and reminders you might require to maintain peacefulness. Come back to the breath.

X

In today's meditation ask how much of your life has been about compromise. What part has been given over to the requirements and desires of others while ignoring your own needs? Has there been a longing to satisfy unmet wishes? If so, let this longing guide you back through the labyrinth, back to your soul's desires. Sit with this for as long as you are engaged in reviewing past relationships starting with childhood. Think of adolescence, student life, young adulthood, marriage, parenting and other responsibilities encountered in life. Ask whether or not any of these compromises changed who you could have been. In writing examine your feelings in connection with any of the situations and be willing to face that you may have made the wrong assumptions about how your life would have turned out, or how it did manifest. Examine how rich your life, in actuality, has become even with all the giving-in and disappointment.

XI

Courage is the most important of all the virtues, because without it you can't practice any other virtue consistently. You can practice any virtue erratically, but nothing consistently without courage.

—Maya Angelou

We all know people who complain and when given a chance, tell you all their troubles. Then there are the people who, when asked how they are no matter what is really going on will say, "Can't complain!" Can't or won't? I'm not talking about the people who state that there is no point in complaining because no one will listen or those who are not in touch with their issues. There are individuals who display an every-day kind of valor, that particular brand of courage summoned on a daily basis, even if it is to just get through that day.

Close your eyes and breathe in. Relax knowing that you possess bravery and can access it more often than you might realize. What does this mean to you?

Think of five times you have been courageous in the last week or month. Remember that there is physical, moral, emotional, psychological and moral strength. How can this information serve you?

Gently come back to the room and begin to write of your feelings and thoughts on the subject. Or, you may want to write a narrative of a particular time when you did answer the call and garnered courage where you thought there was none.

Remember to be gentle and nurturing; this is not a punitive session. You may not beat yourself up because you can't locate the strength sometimes.

XII

The suppression of desire or purpose will thwart the spirit yet drive it to conquer itself if it is remembered that we can be just as motivated by misery as by joy. Sit back now and go to your meditative state. Sit and let your mind wander for a bit. With deep breaths call yourself back and observe where your mind wandered to...did it go to something you are miserable about or to something that promotes joy?

Chances are that your mind may have gone to an area of dissatisfaction, to any area where you didn't do enough or felt that you weren't good enough, productive enough, or... just not enough. Take a look at what bothers you without judging the thoughts. What is it that a magic wand could produce to answer your desire?

Let the misery drive your thoughts to a new destination. Slowly come back to the room and begin to write of how the upset and perhaps even your disgust can lead to a resolution. With compassion for your humanness, with a willingness to honestly look at the problem begin to design a new construct for your solution.

XIII

"The secret in life is enjoying the passing of time." —James Taylor

What do you enjoy? What are you inspired by? Do you match your commitment to well-being with your desires? Or has the feeling of being broken separated you from reconnecting to the well-being you once experienced?

Zen philosophy tells us that the acorn holds the seeds which grow into the tree. Can you now, with eyes closed, picture what your tree of well-being looks like? Can you go through the physical, mental and emotional best picture of how you see your ideal self? I'm not talking about perfect, just your personal best. See yourself as happy and as balanced; see the younger you, full of potential meeting the grown, self-actualizing person you now are. See yourself as you want to be. Come back to the room and write what you have visualized.

XIV THINGS TO SAY EVERY DAY

Remember to say things in the present, as if they are already true:

I love myself and others.

I am in my power.

I am responsible for getting my needs met.

I am at peace.

We are always interpreting the truth the way we see it based on our beliefs. If we remember that there's always another version we open up to non-attachment and peace.

How to achieve and maintain a sense of inner peace?

-meditate

-incubate and nurture peaceful thoughts

-dream

-close your eyes and see it

Close your eyes now and drift in the sea of thoughts the above statements bring about. Sit for as long as you can stay focused. When you find yourself drifting allow yourself to write.

When thoughts are fully expressed drift back and repeat. This is a writing meditation. Repeated as a practice it will strengthen, console and enrich you.

XV

What are your personal needs? Do you have a desire for _________________? Do you give it to yourself? In order to provide security in having what you want or need, you can develop certainty in faith and in trusting the order of life's gifts and lessons.

Draw a blueprint for a balanced life where your personal needs are met, right now. Variety, significance, love and connection are all that is needed. Spiritual growth and a sense of contributing to the world complete the picture for a life of fulfillment, no matter what the circumstances.

Abraham Maslow, the renowned psychologist mentioned earlier in the book suggests that the self actualizing person asks, "How can I serve more completely in this life, with love and joy in my heart?"

Close your eyes now and come to rest. As you breathe deeply and rhythmically be aware of the power you possess to become the architect of your new life. Know that when we seek happiness for ourselves we are left wanting. When we seek it for others we are also fulfilled. Ask how you can contribute to others as a unique expression of yourself; it will contribute greatly to your happiness. Be focused. Be determined. Be compassionate and be vigilant to your new thoughts. Most of society waits for something concrete to happen before they are happy. It is the rarified one per cent who knows the secret: become happy first, the rest will follow.

XVI

Close your eyes and repeat this thought: I am my own savior; I am the only one who can save me, no one else can do it.

Breathe in Internal Freedom.

Give up - expectations, anger, blame and procrastination.

Affirm to just let go and relax.

Resentments and grudges keep us holding on to our past. Write about what you experience from pondering these thoughts.

"Discouragement is the only illness" —George Bernard Shaw

XVII ADDICTION TO PERFECTION

Do you swing from an inadequate self-image to a compulsive drive to be superior? You may be one of the thousands of people who are so afflicted. In today's stressed-out world we tend to put excessive demands on ourselves and others. Are you constantly seeking the excessive approval of others? This concern with being perfect is very manipulative because you tend to think that you are only trying to do a good job.

Sit back and with eyes closed ask how you feel about being worthy just the way you are. Begin to think back to childhood. What thoughts did you entertain about being perfect? What were the messages given to you on this topic at home, at school and within your community? Scan your history regarding this and bring your thoughts up to the present.

Write about your assessment and memories. See if you can make a connection with your current thoughts, beliefs and practices. Are there changes you would like to make? Be careful in your planning as you may fall into a trap of feeling that you must rid yourself of this defect thoroughly and all at once! As with any other healing, be patient and compassionate. Writing, as discussed throughout this book can show you the patterns and pain with compassion, wisdom and love.

Whether you have been overwhelmed, insecure, abused, lonely, depressed, betrayed, manipulated, victimized, isolated, envious, exhausted, hurt, angry, fearful, weak, revengeful, stuck, depleted, frustrated, humiliated, sick or wounded; you can heal!

THE LAST ONE

Malcolm Gladwell, the best selling author and sage has stated that as we gain knowledge and experience we rely on our instincts more. Yet, how many of us in this Google-dominated age sit back, take a breath and ask ourselves what is best?

We often have knowledge without understanding our selves and our lives. In today's world an added layer of complexity often masks our instincts, rendering them inert. Do we remember grandma's home-spun wisdom or do we run out and get the latest "fix-it"?

Come to rest now. Breathe a sigh of relief. You are at home with your wisdom. It has been here all along while you were running around. Welcome home. Be silent and clear your mind. Remember to use the word Sum as you breathe in and Ho as you breathe out if you need an assist to quiet and clear your brain's ramblings. The memory of your higher voice only comes in silence.

Now think of a situation where you are searching for a solution, an answer to what ails you at the moment. Stay out of your own way and let the answer come to you now as an inspiration. An inspiration is simply when an idea takes hold of you. Be home when it knocks. When ready, come back into the room and either write about the process of becoming aware of your intuition or a memory of a time when you used it to great success, perhaps now, and forever more.

RECOMMENDED BOOKS

Beattie, Melody. **Co-Dependent No More.** Center City, MN: Hazelden, 1992.

Bradshaw, John. **Healing the Shame That Binds You.** Deerfield Beach, FL: Health Communications, 2005.

Breathnach, Sarah Ban. **Simple Abundance: A Daybook of Comfort and Joy.** New York, NY: Warner Books, 2001.

Gawain, Shakti. **You Can Heal Your Life.** Navato, CA: New World Library, 2002.

Jampolsky, Gerald. **Goodbye to Guilt.** Bantam Books, 1985.

Monahan, Marta. **The Courage to be Brilliant.** Los Angeles: Vittorio Media, 2002.

Price, Reynolds. **A Whole New Life.** New York: Penguin Group, 1994.

Sarno, John E., M.D.. **Mind Over Back Pain.** New York: Warner Books, 1991.

Schaef, Anne Wilson. **Mediations for Women Who Do Too Much.** Harper & Row, 1990.

Woodman, Marion. **Addiction to Perfection.** Toronto, Canada: Inner City Books, 1982.

Notes

Notes

Notes

Notes

Notes

LaVergne, TN USA
16 February 2011

216578LV00004B/1/P

LV0005487978 3